Praise for

Spiritually Sensitive Caregiving: A Multi-Faith Handbook

"The information is concise and to the point. I am very interested in comparing and contrasting religious beliefs, and to have it all in one easy-to-read form is great!"
Susan Becevra, *MSW – Trauma therapist, Children's Hospital, San Diego*

"It is a quick read and very helpful for busy professionals. I think every nursing student and professor should have a copy."
Sharon Canclini, R.N., MS *– Texas Christian University, Ft. Worth, TX*

"I am extremely impressed with the over-all comprehensive information provided. Not only do I want it on my shelf for referencing but I would highly recommend it to others who work with victims and the social services genre."
Anne Litecky *– Governor's Office of Crime Control and Prevention, Baltimore, MD*

"This book is a resourceful road map to help people become familiar with various religious beliefs and cultural backgrounds. It will help enhance political correctness."
Rev. Dr. Alvin E. Miller *– Pleasant Green Missionary Baptist Church, Nashville, TN*

"I work with Muslim Afghan and Iranians and congratulate you on a job well done on the section on Islam. I am very impressed with your work."
Farid Younos, EdD *– Department of Anthropology and Sociology California State University at East Bay*

"This book is a great primer and reference for me as there is often a long period of time between working with victims other than Christians."
Marti Anderson *– Director Crime Victim Assistance, Iowa Attorney General's Office*

Spiritually Sensitive Caregiving

A Multi-Faith Handbook

By

Janice Harris Lord
Melissa Hook
Sharifa Alkhateeb
Sharon J. English

Spiritually Sensitive Caregiving
A Multi-Faith Handbook

Published by Compassion Press
A division of Compassion Books, Inc.
7036 State Highway 80 South
Burnsville, NC 28714
828-675-5909
www.compassionbooks.com

First printing – March, 2008

Library of Congress Control Number: 2007909846

ISBN-13..............978-1-878321-32-9
ISBN-10............1-878321-32-3

We dedicate this publication to

Sharifa Alkhateeb,

whose contributions to it represent her final work before
she died of pancreatic cancer on October 21, 2004.

Sharifa founded advocacy groups for Muslim women and explained the ways of Islam to America and to the world as a scholar, journalist, and educator. She embraced both the American and the Islamic ways in her lifelong effort to bridge gaps between the two cultures. Sharifa founded the *Peaceful Families Project* at the FaithTrust Institute in Seattle. Often quoted in news reports about Muslim matters, particularly pertaining to women, Sharifa also advised schools, police departments, corporate directors, governmental agencies, and textbook publishers on the nature of Islam.

As founder of the North American Council for Muslim Women, Sharifa Alkhateeb focused attention on domestic violence and other problems of women in the Islamic world. She edited an English translation of the Qur'an, chaired the Muslim caucus at the United Nations World Conference on Women in Beijing in 1995, and helped get Arabic introduced as a subject of study in several public schools in Northern Virginia.

Sharifa Alkhateeb's royalties for the sale of this book are being donated to the *Peaceful Families Project*, administered by her daughter Maha B. Alkhateeb, and the *Muslim Community Center for Human Service's* Domestic Violence Program in Richland Hills, TX.

> — *Janice Harris Lord, Melissa Hook*
> *and Sharon J. English*

Sharifa Alkhateeb

In many ways, Mrs. Alkhateeb lived a conventional Muslim life. She was the mother of three daughters, faithfully prayed five times a day and observed her religion's dietary practices and other customs. Although she wore western dresses and slacks, she covered her hair with a scarf since she was sixteen years old.

Yet within the bounds of her faith, Mrs. Alkhateeb sought—and usually found—a way to forge a strong, independent voice for herself and for other Islamic women. "[We] Muslim women are quite capable of speaking up for ourselves," she told the New York Times in 1993. "We're not waiting for Western women to pour their loveliness into our heads."

After the attacks of Sept. 11, 2001, Mrs. Alkhateeb was "in constant fear that someone would attack her," according to her daughter Maha Buthayna Alkhateeb. But she pinned a U.S. flag to her blouse and took a leading role in the Community Resilience Project of Northern Virginia, a counseling and education effort sponsored by the Federal Emergency Management Agency. She also helped organize an interfaith consortium of synagogues, churches and mosques to educate people across religious and cultural lines.

"She always felt extremely spiritual," her daughter said. "She always felt she was doing what she was meant to do."

Sharifa Alkhateeb was born in Philadelphia, the daughter of a Yemeni father and a Czech mother. Hers was the only Muslim family in a Christian and Jewish neighborhood.

After entering the University of Pennsylvania at 16, she joined the Muslim Student Association and began to wear the scarf. But she did not renounce

American ways or the growing feminist movement of the 1960s.

"She's encountered people who wanted her to stop speaking out ever since the beginning," her daughter said. "She believed in taking the best of both worlds. She didn't see it as a clash of civilizations at all."

After graduating from Penn, Mrs. Alkhateeb received a master's degree in comparative religion from Norwich University in Northfield, VT. She then edited the Marmaduke Pickthall translation of the Qur'an, published in 1977.

From 1978 to 1987, she lived in Saudi Arabia, where her husband, an Iraqi-born U.S. citizen, was working. She taught in private schools and at a Saudi university and worked as a journalist for the English-language *Saudi Gazette*, sometimes receiving warnings for reporting on women and other sensitive issues.

After moving to Northern Virginia in 1988, Mrs. Alkhateeb became a diversity trainer with the Fairfax County public schools, was president of the Muslim Education Council and produced, from 1993 to 1997, a monthly television program for the Fairfax school system, *Middle Eastern Parenting*.

She was co-author of the *Arab World Notebook*, which is used in public schools nationwide, and was managing editor of the *American Journal of Islamic Social Sciences*. She founded the Peaceful Families Project, a nationwide program sponsored by the Department of Justice to examine violence in the Muslim community. Her study found that 10 percent to 12 percent of Muslim families in the United States had episodes of domestic violence.

"She was an educator and activist in the fullest sense of the term," said John L. Esposito, a professor at Georgetown University and an authority on Islamic culture. "Bright, religiously centered and motivated, she balanced a kind, considerate, warm nature with an ability to stand firm for the principles she believed in." She was the first woman to receive the Community Service Award from the Islamic Society of North America.

"I raised my daughters to question everything—to weigh all opinions," Mrs. Alkhateeb once said, "including mine."

– Matt Schudel, *Washington Post,*
Wednesday, October 27, 2004; page B-6
Reprinted with permission

Contents

Preface

Citizens of sixty-two countries were working in the World Trade Center when it was attacked. Among the thousands killed and injured, all of the world's major religions were represented. Without doubt, even outside New York City, the United States is experiencing a dramatic blossoming of religious diversity. And this growth affects not only those who deal with traumatic disasters but all those who care for the sick, the injured, the dying, and the troubled.

What is a caregiver to do when a Hindu woman resists pain medication because she believes suffering will improve her plight in her next life? What is a male caregiver to do when a Muslim woman resists removing her head covering in his presence and thereby makes treating her head wound difficult? These types of dilemmas used to be rare, but now they are commonplace.

The United States is still dominantly Christian. But its "religious diversity has shattered the paradigm of America as an overwhelmingly Christian country with a small Jewish minority," says Diana Eck, who heads up the Pluralism Project at Harvard University. She claims that the United States has become the most religiously diverse nation in the world.[1] This is partly a result of recent immigration patterns.

The total number of immigrants living in the United States reached an all-time high of 37.5 million in 2006, an increase of 16 percent in five years. While much media attention has been given to immigrants from Mexico, nearly 10 million of these immigrants are from Asia,[2] the seat of many religions new to U.S. caregivers.

Perhaps a brief history of recent immigration to the United States will help explain these numbers. In 1965, the Immigration Act eliminated quotas linking immigration to national origin, which opened the door to greater religious diversity than ever before. Each year since then, between 500,000 and one million immigrants entered the United States legally. In 1991, after passage of the Immigration Act of 1990, immigration peaked at two million per year.[3]

Over the last two decades, then, about 24 million immigrants have come into the country, according to a recent Urban Institute Study,[4] and they have filled about three out of every ten new jobs in the United States.[5] The leading native countries of these immigrants include Mexico, Canada, and China. These new residents of

the United States have settled everywhere, but most densely in California, which continues to lead the nation in immigrant population, which is 27 percent of the state's population. New York and Texas rank second and third.[6]

Even after restrictions were imposed on immigration after September 11, 2001, the foreign-born population of the United States increased 2 percent (700,000) in 2001 and 3 percent (one million) in 2002.[7]

The U.S. Department of Veteran Affairs now authorizes 39 different religious symbols, including the Latin cross, the Star of David, the Muslim Crescent and Star, and the angel Moroni, that can be used on headstones.[8]

While the United States does not include a question about religion in its census, various experts have made reasonable estimations. For example, Kosmin and Lachman[9] estimated that between 1990 and 2000:

- The number of Hindus increased by 237% to total more than 1 million in this country.
- The number of Buddhists increased by 170% to also reach more than 1 million living in the United States.
- The number of Muslims more than doubled to over 1 million, with about 65% being foreign-born. However, an Official State Department Fact Sheet cites Power[10] (1998) in stating that Islam is by far the fastest growing religion in the United States and estimates that by the year 2010, the Muslim population will surpass the Jewish population by increasing to 4 to 6 million.

The increasing religious diversity of our nation requires all of us, especially caregivers, to learn about faiths other than their own. As they did on September

11, 2001, professional caregivers from both the secular and faith-based communities find themselves more frequently reaching out to hurting people who have unfamiliar cultural and religious practices. It will take training to ensure that services appropriately address the physical, emotional, social, material, and spiritual needs of those in their care.[11]

This book will help with such training. The authors have worked together with a cadre of consultants and reviewers to include information that is helpful to emergency responders, health care and mental health professionals, educators, law enforcement and other justice personnel, and any others who seek to offer culturally-sensitive services to those in need.

We begin with a chapter on spiritually sensitive caregiving and then explore basic information about the practices of the six largest faith groups in the United States. Each chapter for a faith group includes information about basic beliefs and rituals, death issues, and justice issues.

The six religious paths that we investigate are these:

- Native American spirituality
- Hinduism
- Buddhism
- Judaism
- Christianity
- Islam

We have presented the religious paths in the order of their most commonly accepted dates of origin, although both Native Americans and Hindus often say that theirs is the oldest. Since Native Americans are believed to have entered Alaska from Asia, it is difficult to determine. Rather than discuss the intricacies of each spiritual path, we have focused on basic, concrete information that will help caregivers to interact in ways that enable them to give sensitive and effective treatment.

For simplicity's sake, we have not attempted to go into detail about the differences within subgroups of each religious approach. We did not intend to confuse you, or ourselves, with so much detail that the book became impractical. We want it to help you in your work.

Authors, Consultants, Reviewers

The authors of this handbook wish to thank those from various faiths
and from a variety of professional experiences who have
consulted with us and reviewed this manuscript.

Authors

Janice Harris Lord, MSW, is the author of many books and articles on
trauma, grief, and spirituality in social work practice and victim advocacy.
She is the wife of a Christian minister and served as National Director of
Victim Services for Mothers Against Drunk Driving for fourteen years.
She has been a partner on clergy-training projects and has collaborated on a
seminary curriculum on ministry to victims of crime. Janice is also in private
practice and coordinates a discussion group of women from various faiths
(Daughters of Abraham) in Texas. For this publication, Janice Lord focuses
on Native American Spirituality and Christianity. She also served as primary
editor for the book.

Sharon J. English, MSW, has more than thirty-five years of experience in
the juvenile justice system. She currently serves on the California Youthful
Offender Parole Board as a Hearing Officer. In 1991, Sharon's mother was
murdered by a paroled prisoner she had met through a prison ministry
program. For this publication, she focuses on Judaism and Hinduism.

Melissa Hook, BA, an author who writes about ethics and crime victim
issues, has published in a number of magazines, books, and journals. She
is the Director of the Office of Victim Services of the District of Columbia.
Melissa is a practicing Buddhist and was a special projects editor for *Tricycle:
The Buddhist Review* between 1993 and 1998. For this publication, Melissa
Hook focuses on Buddhism.

Sharifa Alkhateeb, MA, was the president of the North American Council
for Muslim Women and the president of the Muslim Education Council. (See
Dedication pages.) For this publication, Sharifa Alkhateeb focuses on Islam.
This was Sharifa's last work before her death.

Consultants

Catherine Madigan, an award-winning freelance writer and editor in Arlington, Texas, served as the first-line editor for the project. Anne Seymour and Allana Pettigrew also provided technical editing services.

Many other consultants have been crucial to this publication. The authors express sincere gratitude to each of them, including:

Lori Alvard, M.D., Associate Dean of Student and Multicultural Affairs at Dartmouth Medical School and the first female Navajo surgeon in the United States;

Thanissaro Bhikku, an American-born Theravada monk who has been Abbot of the Metta Forest Monastery near San Diego since 1993;

Kenneth Cracknell, Professor of Theology at Brite Divinity School in Fort Worth;

Cary A. Friedman, Rabbi of Congregation Anshe Chesed in New Jersey and consultant with the FBI Behavioral Science Unit;

Marsha Friedman, Attorney and teacher of Judaica and member of Congregation Anshe Chesed in New Jersey;

Ramdas Lamb, Professor of Comparative Religions at the University of Hawaii in Honolulu and a former Hindu Monk;

Ron Lessard, Executive Director of the Baltimore American Indian Center;

Shannon McCaslin-Rodrigo, PhD Postdoctoral Fellow at the PTSD Research Program, University of California, San Francisco;

Ada Pecos Melton, a national consultant on Native American issues and a member of the Pueblo Nation;

Paramacharya Palaniswami, Editor of *Hinduism Today*;

Dr. Julie Patrusky, Counseling Director of Shalom Bayit and Jewish Family and Children's Services in Oakland, California;

Rosie Psosie-Binjham, member of the Navajo Nation, teacher and congressional aide in Arizona;

Gehlek Rimpoche, an incarnate lama born in Tibet who founded Jewel Heart in Ann Arbor, Michigan, and teaches Tibetan Buddhism to western students;

Stan and Phyllis Rosenblatt, survivors of two homicide victims, their son and daughter-in law, and founders of Virginians United Against Crime;

Sharon Salzberg, author and co-founder of the Insight Meditation Society in Barre, Massachusetts, who teaches Vipassana Buddhism;

Venerable Samu Sunim, a Korean Zen master and founder of the Buddhist Society of Compassionate Wisdom; and

Dr. Beth Todd-Bazemore, associate professor in the Native American mental health track of the Clinical Psychology program at University of South Dakota.

Reviewers

Numerous reviewers have added their experience and expertise to make the publication practical for the faith community and the victim assistance community. These reviewers include:

Imam Naadim Abdulkhabiyr, Philadelphia Police Muslim chaplain, affiliated with Majlis ash-Sura;

Mary Achilles, Director of the Pennsylvania Governor's Office of the Victim Advocate;

Fareeha Ahmed, teacher at Sunday Mosque School in Irving, Texas;

Barbara Allen, Victim Witness Coordinator for the State's Attorneys Office in Cumberland, Maryland;

Khatra Ali, Community Organizer with Civil Society in St. Paul and a Muslim from Somalia;

Connie Aligada, member of St. Matthew's Catholic Church in St. Paul;

Marti Anderson, Director of Crime Victims Assistance in the Iowa Attorney General's Office;

Ruth Atkin, Senior Staff Assistant of Aging and Adult Services in Martinez, California;

Peggy Basham, Victim Witness Coordinator of the Baltimore County State's Attorney's Office;

Scott Beard, Project Director for several federal faith-based initiative grants and civil crime victims attorney in South Carolina;

Susan Beccerra, Trauma Therapist at Children's Hospital in San Diego;

Nancy Bell, San Ramon Religious Leaders Association in Concord, California;

J. Bolzar, Director of Northeast Victim Services in Philadelphia;

Jaime Burgas of Juvenile Probation Victim Services in Philadelphia;

Russell Butler, Executive Director of Maryland Crime Victims Resource Center in Upper Marlboro, Maryland;

Sharon Canclini, professor of nursing at Texas Christian University in Fort Worth, Texas;

Anita Barnes Cauthorn of Women in Transition in Philadelphia;

Bonnie Clairmont, member of the Hocak Nation who works at the Tribal Law and Policy Institute in St. Paul; **Kathy Coursey,** Victim Assistance Coordinator of the Howard County, MD, Police Department;

Debbie Creswell, Victim Advocate in the Harford County, MD, Sheriff's Office; **Leslie Davila,** Victim Witness Coordinator of the Philadelphia District Attorney's Office;

Ruth Ann Eide of the St. Paul Police Department;

Lucky Farrah, Legal Advocate with the Domestic Abuse Project in St. Paul and a Muslim from Somalia;

Teresa Ann Forliti of Breaking Free, a victim assistance program for prostitutes in St. Paul;

Beth Friend, freelance radio producer and a member of Beth Jacob Congregation in St. Paul;

Stephanie Frogge, Director of Victim Services for TAPS and graduate of Brite Divinity School in Texas;

Tara Gibson, Victim Advocate at the Maryland Crime Victims Resource Center;

Esther Giller, President and CEO of Sidran Institute for Traumatic Stress, Education, and Advocacy in Baltimore;

Maureen Gilmer of the Anne Arundel County, MD, State's Attorney's Office; **Sylvia Gray**, member of Congregation Beth Shalom in Arlington, Texas;

Anna Grenier, child and adolescent counselor for Women Organized Against Rape in Philadelphia;

Suzanne Guinn, Victim Services Manager for Mothers Against Drunk Driving in Lacey, Washington;

Shirley Haas, Compliance Coordinator with the Maryland Governor's Office of Crime Control and Prevention;

Jennifer Hamernick, therapist with St. Gabriel's System in Philadelphia;

Chhen Heng, a Buddhist victim Witness Advocate in South Philadelphia;

Regina Holtman, member of Rush Creek Christian Church in Arlington, Texas;

Yvette House, Program Manager for the Collaborative Response to Crime Victims Project in St. Paul;

Carol Hughes, Community Education Coordinator for STAND! Against Domestic Violence in Concord, California;

Hope Johnson of San Diego;

Latina Johnson, Prevention Education Specialist at Victim Services Center of Montgomery County, Pennsylvania;

Rev. Helen MC Jones, Tragedy Response Unit support Team in Philadelphia;

Wanda Jones of the Victim Services Program of the First Judicial District Family Court in Philadelphia;

Officer **Michael Kennedy** of the Philadelphia Police Department;

Rizwana Khalid, retired banker and practicing Muslim in Fort Worth, Texas;

Tonya Lapido, therapist with the Anti-Violence Partnership of Philadelphia;

Jeanette Lake-Dooley, Inspector in the Victim Services Division of the Philadelphia Police Department;

Brenda LeMay, Victim Advocate with the Garrett County, MD, Sheriff's Office;

Tami Levin, Victim Services Division of the Philadelphia Police Department;

Sandra Lewis, Director of Counseling at Domestic Violence Center of Chester County, Pennsylvania;

Anne Litecky, Victim Services Coordinator for the Maryland Governor's Office of Crime Control and Prevention;

Richard Lord, pastor of Rush Creek Christian Church in Arlington, Texas;

Captain Thomas Lynch, Victim Services Division of the Philadelphia Police Department;

Jocelyn Martell, crime victim and board member of Parents of Murdered Children in Denver;

Rev. Myra Maxwell, Project Director for the Anti-Violence Partnership of Philadelphia;

Alberta McCargo-James, Juvenile Probation Victim Services Coordinator in Philadelphia;

Rev. Dr. Alvin E. Miller of Pleasant Green Missionary Baptist Church in Nashville;

Linda A. Miller, Executive Director of Civil Society, a crime victims services organization in St. Paul;

Debra Neighoff, Victim Services Coordinator of the Maryland Division of Corrections;

Lashawn Nesmith, Victim Advocate with the First Judicial District in Philadelphia;

Carolyn Nieman, Victim Services Coordinator with the Maryland Division of Parole and Probation;

Marion Odubiyi of the Maryland Coalition for Sexual Assault;

Darlene Protrowski, Victim Advocate with the Crime Victims Center in Erie, Pennsylvania;

Mary Beth Ravenscroft, social worker and elder at Rush Creek Christian Church in Arlington, Texas;

Norma Renville, Executive Director of the Women of Nations/Eagles' Nest in St. Paul;

Terry Rogers, Assistant Director of the Tennessee Office of Criminal Justice Programs;

Roberta Roper, mother of a murdered daughter and veteran crime victim advocate in Upper Marlborough, Maryland;

Valda Rotolo of the Cecil County, MD, Child Advocacy Center;

Shaul Saddick of San Diego;

Sara Rudder, Community Education Organizer for STAND! Against Domestic Violence in Concord, California;

Connie Saindon, Founder and Clinical Consultant with Survivors of Violent Loss in San Diego;

Etta Schmerler, member of Congregation Beth Shalom in Arlington, Texas;

Jim Schmidt, Chief Operating Officer for the Sidran Institute in Baltimore;

Anne Seymour, Senior Advisor with Justice Solutions in Washington, D.C.;

Laura Shaw, therapist with the Marine Family Services Division at Camp Pendleton, California;

Rev. Bryn Smallwood-Garcia, Associate Pastor of Orinda Community Church (United Church of Christ) in Concord, California;

Karleen Smith, retired teacher and member of a Baptist church in Arlington, Texas;

Sally Stabaugh, victim advocate for Mothers Against Drunk Driving in North Texas;

Rabbi George Stern, Northwest Interfaith Movement in Philadelphia;

Karen Strein of the SAFE Program of Catholic Social Services in Philadelphia;

Barbara Strupe, Crime Victim Advocate in Dauphin County, Pennsylvania;

Carole Sturm who identifies herself as a Muslim *and* proud American in Arlington, Texas;

Paul J. Taylor, Senior Pastor at Antioch Christian Center in Pittsburg, California;

Sharon Turner, West County Regional Director if STAND! Against Domestic Violence in Concord, California;

Steve Twist, victims' rights lawyer headquartered in Arizona;

Cheryl Tyiska, Director of Victim Services for National Organization of Victim Assistance (NOVA) in Washington, D.C.;

Katherine Weiss, Staff Attorney with the Senior Law Center in Philadelphia;

Sheila White Eagle, member of the Hocak Nation and Director of the Division of Indian Work with the St. Paul Area Council of Churches;

Shemeka Williams, Victim Advocate with the First Judicial District Family Court in Philadelphia;

Edwin Wood, PhD, English teacher and elder at Rush Creek Christian Church in Arlington, Texas; and

Sharmina Zaman, a practicing Muslim from Fort Worth, Texas.

I
Spiritually Sensitive Caregiving

Spiritually sensitive caregiving is not religious counseling or pastoral care, yet it does call for acute attention to the spirituality of the clients and patients you serve. You may be very skilled at attending to the unique physical, mental, emotional, social, and financial concerns and needs of those you serve, but you may be failing to address the whole person if you avoid inquiry about how your patients' or clients' faith and religious perspectives may be related to what has happened to them. Spirituality forms the root of many people's identity. Consequently, neglecting the spiritual dimension is like ignoring their social environment or psychological state.[1]

Persons of faith who believed they are spiritually protected can react with despair when unfortunate things happen to them or someone they love. Many faithful people base their lives on the belief that good things come to good people and bad things come to bad people. When something bad and undeserved happens, they may no longer be able to trust their former belief system. They may have to reconstruct their theology, or lack of theology, to accommodate what has happened – and that process can be long and challenging.

People can also lose trust in their faith communities. They may be offended by platitudes like, "It was God's will. You'll eventually understand why." They may find themselves abandoned by faith leaders and others in their faith community who avoid them, possibly because they don't know what to say or because they fail to realize that trying to accommodate what happened to one's religious beliefs is a long-lasting arduous task. This lack of understanding can leave a person feeling lonely, isolated, and angry.

Trauma-related deaths like homicides and vehicular crashes, as well as all kinds of injuries perpetrated by another human being, also introduce integrity issues for many survivors. Faith leaders, family, or friends may tell them that they should forgive the offender because this is what God expects of them. Others may be told they need to accept karmic influence. While most people recognize these as noble goals, they simply may not be able to achieve them and be honest with themselves at the same time. They cannot accept what seems unfair and undeserved as divine providence.

Faith leaders sometimes underestimate grief and trauma-related symptoms and over-spiritualize expectations for recovery. Likewise, secular caregivers often fail to be sensitive to spiritual diversity and lack the willingness to determine and make appropriate referrals to the faith community. They must learn enough about the faiths practiced in their communities to ensure that they do no harm by failing to recognize how spirituality can affect or be affected by what happens to people.

Definitions

Many different definitions of faith, religion, and spirituality have been proposed through the ages, but for purposes of this publication, these definitions are used:

- Spirituality refers to one's search for meaning beyond the ordinary human realm, and centers on reality beyond the five senses. A person can be spiritual without being engaged in organized religious practice.

- Religion refers to the organized behavioral manifestation of values and beliefs within a certain form of spirituality. A person can be religious without being spiritual, perhaps valuing the tradition, symbolism, academic aspects, or social interaction of religious practice more than spiritual aspects.

- Faith refers to one's trust in or allegiance to their spirituality and/or religion.

- Soul/Spirit/Consciousness refers to that which transcends the body, that which is the person's true essence.

First Amendment Issues

Unless you are a clergy person, a chaplain, or a hospice worker and your program receives government funding, you may have been told that you should not concern yourself with a client or patient's spirituality because of First Amendment restrictions. The First Amendment issue is confusing to many caregivers.

With varying understandings of the phrase "separation of church and state," the U.S. Supreme Court, primarily since 1947, has addressed the right to public religious expression. The phrase itself is presumed by most people to be in the First Amendment. It is not.

The Amendment states: *Congress shall make no law respecting an establishment of religion or prohibiting the free exercise thereof.*

The Founders showed enormous respect for religion by requiring government to remain as separate from it as possible, and also by guaranteeing its free exercise. Thomas Jefferson wrote, "Religion is a subject on which I have ever been most scrupulously reserved. I have considered it as a matter between every man and his Maker, in which no other, and far less the public, has a right to intermeddle."[2]

Before the 1947 Supreme Court case, Everson v. Board of Education,[3] the Court's attention to religion focused primarily on assuring that no single denomination would be established as the national religion (the Establishment Clause), and that no one would be denied the right to freely exercise the religion of their choice (the Exercise Clause). The intent was not to limit religious expression or activity but to limit the power of government to prohibit or interfere with that expression.[4]

The Everson case was about use of tax dollars for tokens for children to ride buses to Catholic schools in New Jersey. The Court found that this activity was constitutional because it was not contributing to the "establishment of religion on the part of the government." It was not paying money directly to the school but to parents to help them get their children to school. However, in explaining why this practice was not a constitutional breach, Justice Black wrote for the majority that "The wall between church and state must be high and impregnable. We could not approve the slightest breach."[5] From this point forward, the Supreme Court appears to have focused less on protection of the right of religious expression and more on avoiding the mixture of church and state, which might be understood as "establishment" of religion.

The courts continue to make diverse rulings about the establishment issue. A recent example at a lower court level is a case in which U.S. District Judge Gladys Kessler[6] ruled that AmeriCorps volunteers could not be placed in Catholic schools. The Corporation for National and Community Service, which administers AmeriCorps, argued that its funding was awarded based on the program's secular activities rather than the religious teachings and prayer services of the schools. However, Kessler ruled that the government could not monitor the programs to ensure that the activities were mostly secular and therefore, "such direct government involvement with religion crosses the vague but palpable line between permissible and impermissible government action under the First Amendment."

 In 1971, Justice Berger, in Lemon v. Kurtzman,[7] sets a standard that attempts to refine the concerns of separating church and state. It states that laws:

- must create no excessive entanglement between government and religion;
- must have a predominately secular purpose;
- must neither advance nor inhibit religion.

This majority opinion is only about the establishment of laws; however many programs and agencies have applied it to their own policies and procedures.[8] It has been argued that these guidelines rest upon the ability of secular organizations to separate their sacred and secular missions, as large denominational charities (such as Catholic Charities USA and the Salvation Army) have done.[9] For more than 100 years, case law has found that the Establishment Clause of the First Amendment does not bar the provision of direct Federal grants to organizations that are controlled and operated exclusively by members of a single faith.[10]

Saying that religion and the government have lived together and influenced one another in nothing new. Of course they have. From prohibition to abolition to the civil rights movement to the long list of social services available to Americans today, they have worked together to promote liberty and justice for all and still stay within Constitutional guidelines.

With bi-partisan support, the Personal Responsibility and Work Opportunity Reconciliation Act of 1996 (P.L. 104-193) significantly changed the relationship between the faith community and the public sector. It allowed religious organizations to compete for funds on the same basis as secular agencies without impairing the religious character of the organizations, and without diminishing the religious freedom of beneficiaries of assistance funded under such programs. Faith-based organizations are no longer required to establish a separate 501(C)(3) nonprofit organization to receive public funding to provide social programs. However, they must maintain separate accounting systems for the services and must use the funds for the intended social services, not for worship, instruction, or promotion of any single faith.

In January 2001, President George W. Bush established the White House Office of Faith-Based and Community Initiatives to strengthen and expand the role of faith-based and community organizations to address the nation's social problems. Centers were created in six Federal Departments (Justice, Agriculture, Labor, Health and Human Services, Housing and Urban Development, and Education) and four Federal Agencies (International Development, Commerce, Veteran Affairs, and Small Business Administration). These Centers are to:

- Ensure that all non-governmental organizations compete on an equal footing for federal financial assistance;
- Ensure that the federal government does not discriminate against an organization on the basis of religion or religious belief; and
- Ensure that religious organizations may retain their independence and expression of beliefs when administering federal funds (for example, they do not have to remove religious art, icons, scriptures, or other religious symbols) as long as they do not discriminate on the basis of religion, religious belief or practice, or religious character in the administration or distribution of federal funds. Likewise, religious organizations must not use federal funds for

inherently religious activities such as worship, worship instruction, or proselytizing. These inherently religious activities must be offered separately, in time or location, from federally-funded programs or services. [11]

Spiritual Assessment

Not all professional caregiving roles are appropriate for spiritual assessment. Spiritual assessment is suggested only for caregivers who expect a reasonably long-term relationship with a client or patient.

Dr. Harold G. Koenig, Associate Professor of Psychiatry and of Medicine at Duke University Medical Center, educates physicians about how to take a spiritual history, and his guidance may serve others well. He points out that:

- Questions should be brief and take only a few minutes to ask;
- Questions should be easy to remember so they may be asked at the most appropriate time (usually within the context of a social history); and
- Information is all about the patient's (client's) beliefs and has nothing whatsoever to do with the physician's beliefs.[12]

Conducting a brief spiritual assessment may be all that is required for many people. When being asked a few simple questions, some will make it clear that they do not wish to include spiritual concerns in the services they receive. Those who do, however, may feel validated and grateful because you inquired about it in a respectful manner.

Some unassuming questions that may encourage clients or patients to begin talking about their spiritual concerns include:

- "What is most important to you in your life right now?"
- "What has been meaningful and helpful to you as you have coped with what happened?"
- "What has strengthened you as you deal with this?"
- "Do you have a support system as you go through this experience?"

If the responses to these questions are not spiritually oriented, that's fine. You may not want to explore spirituality any further.

If the person's responses are spiritually oriented, continue to explore his or her answers as you would any other information that helps you assess the person's strengths and resources as well as stressors.

If you are comfortable addressing spirituality more directly, you may consider the three questions Dr. Dale Matthews, Associate Professor of Medicine at Georgetown University, asks his patients:[13]

- "Is religion or spirituality important to you?"
- "Do your religious or spiritual beliefs influence the way you look at your problems right now?"
- "Would you like to include your religion or spirituality in the work we do together?"

Obviously, if the answer to the first question is "no," you would not explore it further.

A sense of humility and a spirit of alliance are crucial to this process. Respecting a person's spiritual journey is much more than tolerance. It extends to genuine appreciation of differences, and requires you to seek clarity and to pursue self-education. The wisdom of Mahatma Gandhi may serve us well in this regard. He believed that there is a divine truth that transforms all cultures and religions, and that this truth is beyond the ability of anyone to know completely, given our limitations as human beings. Gandhi's belief may or may not represent your own spirituality, but it does represent an attitude that clients and patients may find helpful as they bring their spiritual concerns to you.

The client's or patient's spiritual perspective must be acknowledged and respected, regardless of your own spiritual perspective. When someone is clearly seeking spiritual "answers," you will generally refer them to a spiritual leader of their own faith. You are not expected to offer "answers" but simply to accompany the person on his or her spiritual journey. A genuine sense of healthy inquiry about spiritual implications should become as comfortable for you as inquiry about other aspects of your client's or patient's experience.

In his book *Spiritual Diversity in Social Work Practice: The Heart of Helping*, Dr. Edward Canda[14] suggests that the first step to spiritually sensitive practice is to pay gentle but keen attention to your own personal reaction when someone brings up a spiritual issue. Does your reaction indicate that you may be biased as a result of your personal history, previous experiences, assumptions, spiritual beliefs and commitments, strengths, or limitations?

Just as it may have taken time for you to develop the ability to listen to clients or patients, it may take time for you to learn to recognize spiritual concerns as a component of the whole person. If you practice strength-based caregiving, a mental health method that guides clients to tap back into strengths and resources that helped them cope in the past, you may find that the greatest source of strength for many people is their spirituality. It has been well recognized that most people turn to their faith communities for help before they turn to secular services.[15]

Dr. Canda[16] has distinguished between four categories of spiritually sensitive practice for social workers. (Adapted from Ethical Considerations for Using Spiritually-Based Activities, used with permission):

Conditions for Determining Spiritual Reactions	Options for Spiritual Reactions
1. Client expresses no interest in spirituality	• Caregiver's relationship with the client may demonstrate spiritual values (respect as one created by God, for example) though not specifically addressed. • Caregiver may engage in private spiritual activity, such as praying for the client at home, but does not further explore spirituality unless the client brings it up.

2. Client expresses interest in exploring spirituality	• The above, plus: • Caregiver may explore spirituality issues to the degree the he or she feels competent. • Caregiver refers client to outside spiritual resources. • With permission, caregiver may collaborate with outside spiritual resource.
3. Client and caregiver have developed a spiritually sensitive relationship	• The above, plus: • Caregiver may accept invitation of the client to attend a religious ritual outside working hours such as a memorial event (paying attention to spiritual and cultural customs about actually participating) • The above, plus • The caregiver has relevant spiritual qualifications such as having completed
4. Clinical Pastoral Education or is an otherwise licensed or certified clergy person or pastoral counselor	• The above, plus: • Caregiver may initiate spiritual activities with caution.

The implication of Dr. Canda's chart is that you simply assess the degree of interest clients have in spirituality and react accordingly. Just as there is a wide range of spiritually sensitive practice, there is also a wide range of reaction as it relates (or doesn't relate) to spirituality.

While a person's spiritual and religious beliefs can be altered or disrupted by traumatic events,[17] you must be careful not to assume that this happens all the time. One person, for example, may be able to accommodate what happened into her religious beliefs, never questioning whether God had a role in it. She may not need to rethink her theology. Another person may find that her beliefs about the world and God are shattered by what happened. She may long to find a way to accommodate it into her belief system. If she experiences panic attacks or develops depression, she may find herself feeling further alienated from her previous faith experience.[18] Her faith community may also reject her if they interpret her symptoms or reactions as lack of faith.

Validating a person's faith experience does not require expertise in the religions of the world, but it does require an understanding of common ways to alienate someone spiritually. With an ironically invalidating title, The Complete Idiot's Guide to World Religions, the book suggests how to avoid errors when seeking information from someone of an unfamiliar faith:[19]

- Don't fixate on "Why?" It is quite possible that the person does not know the ultimate reasons for a particular practice and may presume the question has unfriendly intent.
- Don't hold the person responsible for recent bad press generated by a representative of his or her faith.
- Don't refer to a believer as "typical" or "normal." There is no one and only way to categorize spiritual or cultural issues.
- Don't use polarizing language like "sect," "cult," "recruit," "programming," or "variant." Likewise, don't ask sensitive questions that have nothing to do with your work with a particular patient or client; for example, asking Christian Science practitioners why they don't engage in contemporary medical treatment or asking Mormons why some practitioners of their faith accept polygamy.
- Don't pretend to have all the answers.

Culture and Spirituality as Diversity Issues

Spiritually sensitive caregiving requires that you be able to recognize when a client or patient is experiencing a crisis of faith and react with respect and willingness to explore it. This is very difficult without basic knowledge of the faiths in your community. It also requires that you seek to understand how culture and ethnicity interact with spirituality because, in nearly every case, they are intertwined. At a minimum, most religions seek to influence culture in a moral way.

Religion and culture form synergisms that can be confusing. Because they so often go hand in hand, stereotyping and conflict can result when distinctions are not made. For example, spiritual practices of traditional Native Americans living on reservations can differ widely from those of Native Americans who have left the reservation and have become urbanized and evangelized by Christians.

Another example is criticism of Islam since September 11, 2001. Many critics fail to distinguish Islamic beliefs from the cultural practices of countries with large Muslim populations or recognize that small groups of extremist Muslims do not represent the basic beliefs of Islam. To draw conclusions without exploring the facts is like evaluating Christianity on the attitudes and behaviors of the Ku Klux Klan, David Koresh, or Jim Jones. Many Muslims point out that it is crucial to distinguish incidents of cultural and political violence from the core teachings of the faith.[20] The Federal Bureau of Investigation (FBI) reported that hate crimes against Muslims in the United States soared from 28 in 2000 to 481 in 2001, an increase of 1700 percent.[21] The American-Arab Anti-Discrimination Committee, which believes it may have been a more natural organization to which these crimes might be reported, claims that during the first nine weeks after September 11, 2001, more than 700 violent incidents were perpetrated against Arabs, Muslims, or those perceived to be Arabs or Muslims.[22] The FBI states that most of these incidents were against people believed to have been of Middle Eastern ethnicity, and that the offenders mistakenly confused ethnicity with religion. Imam A. Malik Mujahid, chair of the Council of Islamic Organizations of Greater Chicago recently brought this point home by stating that 28,000 Muslims were detained after 9/11, but by 2007 only 39 of them had been formally charged or convicted of a crime.[23]

The length of time immigrants have lived in this country may influence their reaction to things that happen to them.[24] Generally, the more recently they came to the United States and the nearer they are to their homeland, the more likely immigrants' beliefs and practices will be affected by their traditional culture. People who speak their native language at home generally tend to adhere more to traditional cultural and spiritual beliefs and practices than those who have learned English and speak it at home.[25]

Previous experiences of oppression and violence due to cultural, religious, or political beliefs can also play a role in how they react to troubling events. Political refugees who have suffered at the hands of law enforcement or governmental sponsored oppression in their native countries, or those living in neighborhoods plagued by police bias, are often skeptical of secular programs and agencies. They may be more likely to turn to their faith communities for help. In The Color of Justice,[26] Brian Ogawa writes, "How immigrant and refugee communities generally perceive justice is a principal factor in determining how to best help them." Caregivers must be aware of the potential for fear and distrust when seeking to help these people.

Referral, Consent, and Confidentiality

To offer spiritually sensitive service, you will need to identify people in your community who represent the spiritual and cultural groups to be served, such as volunteers or spiritual leaders who are known and trusted in the community. Participants in the Victim Services 2000 Program in Denver, Colorado point out that these "gatekeepers" may not be official or recognized community leaders or traditional agency heads, but may have established relationships with those you are trying to help. These gatekeepers can usually be identified by asking community members who they would likely turn to for help in a time of trouble.

In attempting to provide quality professional services to those who are seeking spiritual "answers," you must first evaluate your own expertise. If you are not educated in theology, you can conduct a brief spiritual assessment, can learn about how the spirituality of the client or patient is helping or hindering their healing or recovery, and can help them sort out options for dealing with spiritual issues. However, you should not provide theological explanations or impart religious theology. Instead, you should refer to appropriate spiritual resources you know and trust to be competent and compassionate.

Chaplains who are certified by the Association of Professional Chaplains[27] generally practice in hospitals and have been educated to meet the spiritual needs of a wide variety of people who are suffering. Members of the American Association of Pastoral Counselors (AAPC),[28] likewise, have received both theology and counseling education. Certification in either group means that an individual has completed four years of college, three years of theology school, and one to four years of Clinical Pastoral Education followed by written and oral board certification.

While these individuals may be the most appropriate referral sources, pastoral counselors of the victim's faith and culture also may be consulted. However, not every pastor who counsels is a pastoral counselor. Many who identify themselves as pastoral counselors have received no formal education in counseling at all, so it is important to ask.

It is not necessary to seek consent to include a spiritual assessment in the social assessment or other general inquiry aimed to support the whole person. However, anything beyond spiritual assessment and support requires the informed consent of the client or patient. This includes written consent before discussing his or her situation with a faith leader, teacher, parish nurse, chaplain, or spiritual/pastoral counselor.

Issues surrounding confidentiality can get complicated for those who are both faith leaders and licensed counselors. These individuals must be careful to avoid dual relationships (separating pastoral and counseling functions) with their followers. A recent Texas case involved a faith leader who was both a Christian pastor and a Licensed Professional Counselor (LPC). In a counseling relationship, a woman in his congregation revealed information about her marriage to him and alleged that he later revealed this information to the church board and congregation, directing them to avoid contact with the woman "until the time of repentance and restoration." By doing so, he ignored well-established ethical standards for both Licensed Professional Counselors in the State of Texas and pastoral counselors. The woman filed suit against the pastor and it is still moving through the courts with the 2nd Court of Appeals finding that, as a Licensed Professional Counselor, the pastor is accountable to professional standards for confidentiality established by the Texas Professional Counselors' Act.

The Code of Ethics of the American Association of Pastoral Counselors (AAPC) states: We do not disclose client confidences to anyone except as mandated by law (in most states, this includes child and elder abuse or situations in which the client is in immediate danger to self or others); in the course of civil, criminal or disciplinary action arising from the counseling where the pastoral counselor is a defendant; for purposes of supervision or consultation; or by previously obtained written permission.

You must know and respect state confidentiality laws that apply to you. Likewise, faith leaders with certification or licensing credentials in counseling are bound by confidentiality standards. You should refer only to faith leaders who maintain confidentiality unless the client or patient releases him or her from that standard.

Summary

Spirituality and religious practice are strengthening factors in the lives of many people. Supporting them with spiritually sensitive services validates them and often enhances their recovery.

Other people, however, find that their traditional religious beliefs and practices are more hurtful than helpful following crises in their lives. Helping them consider options to address these painful issues can be very useful.

Still others have no spiritual perspectives to their lives and should not have spiritual expectations placed on them.

The focus of this chapter has been on how to conduct a brief spiritual assessment, how to respect and support a client's or patient's faith and cultural perspective, and how to refer to appropriate spiritual leaders when the assistance needed is beyond the expertise of the caregiver. The authors trust that you will take this information as only the first step. Developing a better understanding of what is happening spiritually with a client or patient is achieved through ongoing gentle, respectful inquiry.

The Handbook

The remainder of this handbook introduces you to the six most widely practiced faiths in the United States, beginning with Native American Spirituality which is believed to be the most ancient of the traditions described. The publication is not intended to be exhaustive. Throughout the centuries, spiritual leaders and practitioners have written volumes about various faiths. The authors of this handbook attempt only to include basic information that will help develop spiritually sensitive services.

It is important to recognize that beliefs and practices are not universal within any religion. It is impossible, for example, to describe the Protestant Christian view or the Muslim view. A spiritually sensitive caregiver must balance the basic elements of a religious tradition with the context of each patient's or client's personal or individual faith.

As you read this handbook, you will find contrasts in the beliefs of the religions addressed, but you also will find surprising commonality among their core values. Each faith tradition, for example, believes that every individual has inherent dignity and worth and deserves positive regard. Similarly, the values that underlie human services work, including service, social justice, and the dignity and worth of every human being, are also valued by each religion.

Things I want To Remember From This Chapter:

2
Native American Spirituality

This brief description of Native American Spirituality is not intended to be exhaustive. The authors recognize that within each faith there are divergent viewpoints. While we respect each individual's beliefs, it is impossible to represent all viewpoints in this limited forum. Therefore, the following information should serve only as a starting point for engaging Native American clients or patients.

Some anthropologists claim that the first Indians came to North America about 25,000 years ago. Others link the first Indians in South America with archaeological sites dating back 50,000 years. However, oral history of each tribe's unique creation story tends to suggest that Native Americans were "put here" by the Creator or were always here[1] and attuned to one Creator God. For example, the beginning for the Kiowas was a struggle for existence in the bleak northern mountains. It was there, they say, that they entered the world through a hollow log.[2]

Each Native American tribe has its own language, culture, and spirituality that evolved from a quest for a harmonious relationship with the environment including natural resources, animals, and other human beings. For example, Indians in the desert Southwest based their practices on agricultural subsistence. Pacific Northwest Indians fished from the sea. Alaskan Indians gathered food from tundra, island, and marine life. Inland Northeastern tribes farmed and hunted game. Even within the tribes, however, spirituality is not a codified, uniform system because each person, with constraints, defines the spiritual for himself or herself.

In the mid-1800s, Manifest Destiny, the political philosophy of the United States held that it was destined to or deserved to conquer the heart of North America from the Atlantic Ocean to the Pacific Ocean. This belief significantly and dramatically altered Indian spiritual traditions, moral structure, and language. Native American lands, culture, and community were taken over by those who felt that they had a right to it. The federal government weakened Indian spirituality by making it illegal to perform their traditional ceremonies. Later, Native American spirituality was again significantly impacted when tribal people were relocated and reeducated between the 1950s and the 1970s. Many Native American children and young people were taken from their families and placed in government, Christian, and Mormon mission schools which intended to de-Indianize, convert, and assimilate them into mainstream culture.

U.S. Senator Ben Nighthorse Campbell, from Colorado, a chief in the Northern Cheyenne Tribe, has pointed out that after centuries of extermination, relocation, disease, and neglect that resulted in the near-extinction of Native Americans a century ago, the Indian and part-Indian population has risen to more than 4 million.

More than 200,000 Americans who identify themselves as fully Native American or American Indian are distributed among 562 federally recognized tribes. Hundreds more may not be officially recognized. Many different tribes may be represented within a given community. For example, the Indian population of Wichita, Kansas includes 4,763 people from 86 different tribes.[3] While practices are diverse, all tribes share the view that each element of creation is sacred, including humans, plants, animals, minerals, and the spirit world. As the Dakota/Lakota spiritual leader Black Elk queried, "Is not the sky our father and the earth our mother; and are not all living things with feet or wings or roots their children?" [4] Native Americans who practice their traditional spirituality believe in the sacredness of all people and respect their individual spiritual beliefs. They see no need to seek converts.

As Native Americans moved into urban areas, the absence of nature weakened their holistic spiritual traditions. Many traditional values governing family relationships also were damaged or destroyed.

The reservations destroyed the foundations of the Indian way of life. The government warred on spiritual beliefs and practices, the authority of the chiefs, and on the tribes themselves, which had provided the political setting and kinship ties that held people together in meaningful relationship. In exchange, the government offered unsatisfying substitutes: plows, work oxen, log houses, schools, and Christianity along with alien ideas of how human beings should behave.[5]

While Christian missionaries on the reservations preached about values that were in sync with Native American values (i.e., be good to your neighbor, help one another, be kind to one another, do not steal), Native Americans could not understand why many who taught these principles behaved differently. For example, Native Americans were already deeply spiritual people who shared what they had with those who needed it. The taking of their land and people by force was foreign to them and in direct opposition to what they were hearing proclaimed. Many of them knew that the Constitution of the United States guaranteed religious freedom, and yet they were denied the right to practice their traditional rituals. The same missionaries who forbad them from performing these rituals took their children from them and put them in Christian boarding schools.[6]

As traditional codes of behavior of Native American families and communities were replaced by western cultural practices, the tribes were left with an incomplete and confusing moral structure by which to address problems. For example, traditional codes had never been put in place to protect women and children against sexual violence because they were not needed. On the reservations, however, alcoholism (which was introduced by fur traders), child abuse and neglect, family violence, and sexual assault emerged as new problems among Native Americans. Even today, tribal justice systems have few traditional remedies to address these crimes. Those who do develop remedies tend to prefer talking circles and banishment to common justice practices in the United States. Native Americans do not understand talking circles as mild sanctions. They require accountability of offenders to their victims and acceptance of punishment. Spiritually sensitive service requires knowledge of and respect for the profound grief experienced by Native Americans for the loss of their land, culture, tradition, language, and spirituality. While many Native Americans today share the cultural and spiritual values of mainstream America, others continue to live in the shadow of their losses. Fear and anxiety about government intervention, programs, and the criminal justice system may cause them to be hesitant to discuss their beliefs, traditions, ceremonies, and activities with non-Indians.

Some tribes protect the identity of their medicine men/women, bar tourists from attending their ceremonies and dances, and resist speaking to outsiders about their spirituality. They feel that too much has already been lost. They are hesitant to share because they are afraid they may lose their traditions once again as they did in the past.

The first step a spiritually sensitive caregiver serving Native Americans might consider is to identify a spiritual advisor from the tribe or tribes in the community and enlist their trust and support. It is crucial to recognize Native American values and perspectives. For example, being attuned to the present moment and appreciating all aspects of the environment may be more important to Native Americans than arriving on time or keeping an appointment. They may not understand the dominant culture's preoccupation with rigorous scheduling, which can be frustrating to caregivers who do not share their perspective. Long silences are considered sacred time to many Native Americans. Most listen well and will respect others who do the same.

Basic Beliefs and Rituals

Supreme Being

- Common themes among all tribes are belief in a deity, generally referred to as Creator, the existence of Spirit, the importance of rituals in communicating with the Spirit, and a deep reverence for all of life.

- The Creator is supreme and inseparable from creation and the larger universe. The Creator is within all things human and non-human, as well as within the spiritual energy that flows among them.

- The universe is often referred to as the Spirit world, whereas life on earth is referred to as the Physical world. The Creator may be referred to as Father, Grandfather, or Great Spirit. The earth may be referred to as Mother.

  - Tribes have their own names for the Creator. For example, Lakotas use the term Wakan Tanka (the Great Mysterious One or the Great Spirit).

  - Cheyennes call God above Heammawihio and God below Ahktunowihio.

Images and Symbols

- There is no image to embody the Creator; however the eagle may symbolize the Creator in the context of creation, or serve as the messenger of the Creator.
  - Father Creator and Mother Earth may be symbolized by blue and green respectively.
  - Blue may also represent water and green may represent earth.
- Geographic areas, such as mountains and lakes, may symbolize the universe. Everything in the universe is considered a gift and is holy.
- The circle is a common symbol among all Native American tribes that represents the unending, circular nature of spirit life.
  - One manifestation of the circle used in some tribes is the Medicine Wheel or Sacred Hoop, which is a circle with a cross in the middle representing the four directions. The four colors of humankind (red, yellow, black, and white) may be used in the quadrants of the circle. The four directions may also be represented by these colors. In some tribes, red represents east, yellow represents south, black represents west, and white represents north. The four colors may also represent the four aspects of one's nature: physical, mental, emotional, and spiritual.
  - Tribal renditions of the Wheel or Hoop vary. For example, within the circle of the medicine wheel of the Seneca tribe is the great tree of peace that brings the six nations of the Iroquois together.

Scriptures/Sacred Texts

There is no Native American holy book. Native American Spirituality is an oral tradition passed down through songs, drumming, and dance. Each tribe has its own spiritual beliefs and leaders whom they revere. Oral tradition has deteriorated over time and what remains is fragmentary (mythology, legend, lore, and hearsay), but the truths underlying the stories remain crucial and complete.[7]

A Native American classic is the book Black Elk Speaks, originally published in 1932 after the Oglala Lakota Holy Man, Black Elk, revealed his revelations to John G. Neihardt (Flaming Rainbow).[8] It has become a guide to North American tribes.

Basic or Core Beliefs

- Native American spirituality is not so much about events in historical time as it is about living with respect for the land, living in harmony within a specific community, and honoring spiritual leaders who have special healing powers within the community.[9]

- Visions and spiritual communication with ancestors are considered sacred among Plains tribes. Spirits of the dead offer wisdom and guidance to the living through prayer and spiritual rituals. Vision Quests are individual spiritual retreats from ordinary life during which a Native American goes into the hills to pray and fast for up to four days and four nights. Quests are periods of individual sacrifice where the individual seeks spiritual connection to the Creator and to ancestors.

- Most tribes recognize the spiritual aspect of dreams and seek to understand them. Some individuals may not share dreams with outsiders until they are first discussed with spiritual leaders within the tribe.

- Physical nature and human nature are not distinct. It is all part of the same whole, and each shares responsibility for the other. In honoring all of Creation, ancient Native Americans attributed supernatural powers to people, birds, animals, plants, and other natural objects. Prayer does not focus on the objects themselves but on their supernatural powers.[10]

- Native Americans seek to live in balance with nature. Human beings do not exist alone but in relation to all Creation. In the Spirit world, the connection to all things is remembered and honored. In the Physical world, it is more difficult to remember. The goal of rituals and ceremonies is to make this reconnection.

- Valuing the interconnection of all living things contributes significantly to mindfulness, helpfulness, and carefulness in relationships with others. This interconnectedness creates a strong sense of community.

- Traditional Native American prayer is spontaneous with little or no dependence on written or memorized prayers.
- In traditional Native American thinking, all of Creation is to be appreciated and shared. For example, the concept of land ownership was a totally foreign concept when white men started claiming it as their own. To Native Americans, land, air, water, and other elements of Creation were given by the Creator and are for the use of all.
- Rather than ownership of goods and materialism, a Native American is taught to exercise stewardship over all things. Native Americans respect and appreciate nature rather than assume superiority over it.
- Early Indian warfare was common, but probably no more so than among the Europeans who came to this country. They returned violence with violence for self-preservation. The white man's publications about Indians as savage beasts were generally exaggerated; the same is true for media stereotyping as radio, movies, and television developed.

Spiritual Leaders

- The roles of spiritual leaders vary among the tribes. Usually the primary spiritual leader is referred to as a medicine man or woman. This person is believed to have special spiritual gifts and is responsible for maintaining a healthy spiritual life in the community.
- Elders are respected leaders who lead and anchor the community.
  - In some tribes, spiritual leaders are identified when they are young or even prior to their birth. They are raised and trained to become spiritual leaders.
  - The medicine person and other tribal leaders, such as council members and hereditary chiefs, are considered servants of the community.

- Native American holy places are designated within the natural setting of the environment: mountains and streams, rivers and lakes, valleys, deserts, highlands, plains, woodlands, and icelands. Most ceremonies take place within nature.

- Most traditional Native Americans do not worship in specific houses of worship. In urban areas, they may conduct ceremonies in apartments, homes, urban Indian centers, or anywhere large enough to accommodate the ceremony.

- Some tribes use structures made from elements in nature.

  - Longhouses are used for spiritual practices by Senecas.

  - Sweat lodges and kivas are considered sacred environments among some tribes. Their purpose is for cleansing, which enables the individual to reconnect with the spiritual world and receive spiritual revelations. A pit is dug for heated rocks, and a structure of tree limbs is erected to form the skeleton over which a tarp and blankets are laid to make the lodge totally dark. The sweat lodge is constructed so that the individual can feel like he or she is in the mother's womb or the center of Mother Earth. Water is poured over the hot rocks at different intervals to bring out the sweat of the participants. By co-mingling one's own lifeblood (sweat) with Mother Earth, a person is believed to be cleansed and strengthened. The inipi is a Lakota sweat lodge used for spiritual practices.

  - The hogan is a Navajo structure for spiritual practices. Males practice in a teepee-shaped hogan made of tree trunks and earth, while females practice in an octagon-shaped hogan made of logs and packed with adobe.

Worship Days(s) of the Week.

None are set aside. All days and all times are considered sacred.

Special Days/Dates/Anniversaries

Ceremonies are planned in relation to the lunar cycle rather than fixed days. They are based on need: healing ceremonies for individuals, thank you ceremonies for spiritual leaders, burial ceremonies, and wedding ceremonies. Little advance notice may be given prior to a ceremony or sacred dance. Often, this notice is disseminated by word of mouth.

Prohibitions

Prohibitions include harming oneself, others, or nature, except in self-defense or for preservation of the tribe.

Images, Symbols and Sacred Ceremonies Unique to Various Tribes

- Northern Plains Indians (Arapaho, Ogala Sioux, Cheyennes)
  - The Sun Dance is the most sacred of ceremonies, its purpose being to engage the dancer with the spirit world. For the good of the community, a few sun dancers dance for four days and four nights without food or water in order to enter the spirit world to receive wisdom. Sun dancers pray for their people, children, elders, and their way of life. They connect to the Tree of Life with a rope like the umbilical cord and are ritualistically reborn at the end of the ceremony. On the fourth day, each male dancer is pierced through the skin of the chest with a blade or sharp skewer and a wooden peg is inserted to represent the pain of birth. Female sun dancers are not pierced because they have endured the pain of childbirth. This dance is held annually in the summer. Sun dances are closed to everyone but the families of the dancers.[11]
  - The Yuwipi or "Spirit-Calling" ceremony is also most commonly confined to the reservation. It involves the observant being wrapped and tied up in a special blanket in a totally darkened room or enclosure while holy persons call the spiritual world to communicate with the individual. Spirit beings enter in the form of blue or blue-green lights that whirl through the room.[12]

- Lakota Sioux
  - Sacred Pipe smoking was introduced many years ago by the appearance of the Buffalo Calf Woman who described where to find the sacred red stone from which to make the pipes. Pipes are universally understood as spiritual. Pipes are filled with the bark of the red willow, called kinnick kinnick, for smoking. It is non-hallucinatory. Prayers are placed in the bowl of the pipe, and when the pipe is smoked, the prayers ascend to the Creator. Because of the Buffalo Calf Woman's appearance, most Native American tribes honor the role of women as spiritual leaders and medicine people. Among the Sioux, the older a woman becomes, the more powerful she is, and her acquired wisdom is honored. She holds the peace pipe when spirits are called.[13] Preparing the tobacco and inhaling the smoke are believed to be means of reconnecting with the spirit world. The smoke represents the physical breath and stands for truth. While smoking, the individual is expected to engage in truthful words, truthful actions, and a truthful spirit.

- Navajos
  - Navajo Sand Paintings are important parts of religious ceremonies intended to convey wisdom. Paintings are begun in the morning and destroyed at the end of the day. They may represent sacred plants and animals, or beings of a higher order or ancient ones.

NOTE: Caregivers need to be aware of pan-Indian charlatans who imitate Indian practice and peddle it for a profit. They are generally not enrolled members of any tribe but identify themselves as healers, shamans, chiefs, or other titles without having received the rigorous and long-term training that tribal medicine people and spiritual leaders complete. Beware of ads on websites or in the Yellow Pages, as most genuine Native American spiritual leaders are very humble and resist drawing attention to themselves. Genuine holy persons have subdued their own egos, with the men having come to appreciate their feminine side and women having come to appreciate their masculine side. Elders or holy persons would not instruct such people to go into communities and offer ceremonies for profit.

Death and Dying Issues

As Native Americans have assimilated into modern culture, they have adopted more mainstream death and burial practices. Christianity, as well as state laws regarding embalming and burial, now permeate and influence Indian death and burial practices. On the other hand, many who seek to practice traditional spirituality try to include traditional beliefs and practices into their death and dying rituals.

Death Notification

- Death notifiers should proactively identify the appropriate spiritual leaders or natural helpers in the tribal community so that when a death occurs, they can be enlisted to help notify and support the family. These persons may be elders or respected professionals.

- Some Native American tribes are matrilineal, such as the Navajo and the Seneca, and some are patrilineal, such as the Lakota. Therefore, it is important to know if the mother or the father is the family leader because the death notification should be given directly to this person.

- In some tribes it will be appropriate to privately deliver the notification to the family leader. In other tribes, it will be appropriate to bring the family together to notify them as a group.

- Among the Navajo, it is important to speak with the family in indirect terms if a victim is near death. Saying specifically that a person is likely to die is believed to be predictive, i.e. thinking or speaking it into reality.

Anatomical Donation

- Native Americans generally do not agree to anatomical donations because they want their loved ones to go to the spirit world with their bodies intact.

- Some tribe members keep body parts, such as gallstones, appendices, and amputations after removal because they believe that others who gain possession of the parts could use them in harmful ways.

Autopsy

- Many Native Americans distrust the medical profession, which may carry over into concerns about autopsy.

- If an autopsy is required, it is important to ask the family if they have concerns about cutting the body. They may have spiritual concerns or worry about what will happen to body parts. If cutting the body is required, Native Americans may conduct rituals that will make the cutting more acceptable.

Body Preparation

- Attitudes about preparation of the body vary among tribes. Most leave preparation to a funeral home, but some will want to assist by dressing their loved one, preparing hair, etc.

  - Lakotas have the body embalmed and may keep it at the home or the community hall until time for burial.

  - Lakotas and Dakotas paint the deceased's feet.

  - Navajos do not touch or prepare the body after death. They believe that what was positive and good in that person is now moving on toward the spirit world, and what was bad or potentially evil is left behind in the body. The body is not taken to the home. They believe that evil spirits may take possession of dead bodies; therefore, they avoid contact and do not visit gravesites.

  - Apaches do not speak the deceased's name and, similar to the Navajos, believe that contact with the body can call back the spirit, which they avoid.

Funeral Practices

- Lingering spirits are of concern to some tribes if the death was untimely, violent, mysterious, or suicidal. Many rituals are ceremonies are designed to help these souls find peace and rest.

- Burials do not take place until four days have passed, giving the departing spirit time to arrive in the spirit world. Navajos and some other tribes do not speak the name of the dead during these four days because they believe it may call his or her spirit back to the body.

- Some tribes hold wakes and ceremonies during the four days before the body is buried.

- Among Lakotas, grieving the loss is formal and openly expressed among the extended family. People speak about the individual and share stories about his or her life.

Burial Practices

- Most Native Americans are buried in the earth rather than cremated. They may be buried with special medals they have received (war veterans) or sacred objects such as eagle feathers or beads.

- Death is understood to be the fulfillment of a person's destiny as the body returns to the dust of the earth once again to contribute to the cycle of natural life.

- Native Americans generally bury their dead in cemeteries.
  - It is important to Navajos that bodies of loved ones be returned to and buried in the diamond-shaped land around their sacred mountain, where they believe they will have extra protection.

- Caregivers who have established a relationship with a Native American family generally are welcome to attend the funeral and mourning activities following the burial; however, ask permission before doing so.

- Lakotas, Hochunks, and other tribes formally address the loss of a loved one once a year on the anniversary of the death for four years. These ceremonies are directed towards the survivors to help them relinquish their attachment to the departed. Lakotas believe that the living can hold back the dead from full entry into the spirit world.
  - At year one, the deceased is believed to be half way into the Spirit world. A ceremony is intended to wipe the family's tears away and remind them that their loved one's spirit is still alive.

- At year two, a ceremony acknowledges that the survivors are rejoining the circle of life.

- At year three, a ceremony formalizes the adoption of another member of the community to replace the relationship with the departed as a means of honoring valued aspects of the departed.

- At year four, a ceremony commemorates the end of grieving and the completed journey to the spirit world.

Views of the Afterlife

- Native Americans generally do not describe the afterlife as a place. They have no concept of hell although, both in this life and after its return to the spirit world, a person remembers that immoral acts such as robbing from Mother Earth or causing unnecessary suffering were committed.

- Native Americans are not greatly concerned about crossing over into the hereafter because they believe the deceased person's spirit is just as alive after death as it was when it lived in the body. While the body is no longer present, the person is still spiritually and emotionally present. On the other hand, grief and sorrow over the absence of the body are understood as natural and cleansing for surviving family members and friends.

  - Lakotas believe that all humanity comes from the Spirit world and returns to it, fully recognizing again their connection to all things. The spirit world is not seen as a new, previously unexperienced paradise but a returning to a way known before.

  - Navajos believe that all things pure return to their original source. The bodily remains are impure and to be avoided.

Justice Issues

American Indians are the victims of violent crime at more than twice the national average. Unlike the situation among Whites and Blacks where the large majority of crime victims are of the same race, 70 percent of crimes against Indians are committed by a person of a different race, 60 percent of them White.[14] These figures are generally believed to under-represent actual crime because of inadequate reporting between reservation citizens and the police agencies, the Bureau of Indian Affairs (which oversees only 28 percent of the law enforcement agencies in Indian Country) and the FBI.

Native Americans practiced the individual freedoms honored in America today long before the white man's arrival on the continent. Holding spirituality close, Native Americans practiced freedom of religion, freedom of speech, freedom of speech in council (open assembly), the right of all tribal citizens, including women, to vote, the privilege to remove an elected leader, and a governing system based on ecology.[15]

Even though these freedoms were eventually taken from them, contemporary Native American spirituality still directly influences their attitudes about criminal justice. In the Native American worldview, there is a deep connection between justice and spirituality; harmony and balance are essential to both.[16] For example, circle sentencing, sometimes called peacemaking circles, emerged from First Nation communities in Canada. Circles include large numbers of victims, offenders, family members, and the justice officials. They pass a talking piece around to assure that each person's perspective is heard, and then decide as a group what needs to be done to restore harmony. Today, these circles are not only used in some tribal courts but in a variety of settings, including large urban areas, for minor criminal and juvenile cases.[17]

A cherished Native American value is that when one harms another, he or she must seek to make it right with the victim or the victim's family. Current restorative justice principles that call for direct accountability to the victim, balanced with interests of the offender and the community is, in many ways, Native American in origin. Following is an example of Lakota justice.

A few years ago, the sacred Lakota sweat lodges on the periphery of a mixed community in South Dakota were destroyed by a group of high school students, devastating the local tribe. The city police were lackadaisical about holding the youths accountable. Their attitude seemed to be, "Who cares about some primitive buildings and a few eagle feathers." The youths were eventually charged, however, and found guilty of the crime. A spiritual leader of the tribe was called upon to advise the judge at the sentencing. He recommended that the youths be required to rebuild the sweat lodges under his watch as a spiritual exercise. This experience developed close relationships between the spiritual leader and the young people, and a new level of respect for Lakota traditions evolved in the community.[18]

These restorative justice concepts may not always be appropriate for violent offenders, but it must be recognized that violent crimes such as child abuse and rape were uncommon in traditional Native American communities before the latter part of the 20th century. This was because codes of acceptable behavior between family members and neighbors were clearly defined and codified, thus negating the need for sanctions. In the Navajo tribe, for example, to avoid manifestations of innate conflict, young wives were never to speak to their fathers-in-law, and young husbands were never to speak to their mothers-in-law.

Today, in the United States, three types of government exist: the Federal justice system, State and Local justice systems, and the Tribal justice system, which includes about 175 tribal courts.

The historical injustices perpetrated on Native Americans in the early history of the United States, when they were relocated to reservations and forced to live in environments unfamiliar and hostile to them, have been likened to prisoner of war camps.[19] Therefore it is easy to understand why they continue to resist Federal and State governance as practiced outside Indian country. The strong adversarial features of the American justice system are dissonant with the communal nature of most tribes.[20]

In 1934, the Indian Reorganization Act allowed tribes to organize their own governments by drafting their own constitutions, establishing their own court systems, and adopting their own laws through Tribal Councils. In recent years, reservation law and order has changed as tribal governments have assumed a more active role, but the shift to a satisfactory system of tribal justice is still far from complete. While some tribal justice systems are very similar to the Federal and State systems, others are not. For example, the New Mexico Pueblos have developed more traditional courts based on Native American values. These courts utilize inclusive decision-making rather than adversity. The Navajo Peacemaker Court was developed in 1982 by the

Judicial Conference of the Navajo Nation to provide a forum for traditional mediation. The process relies on elders who are committed to reaching a workable solution rather than an impartial judge or jury passing judgment.

Among the most troubling issues to all law enforcement personnel in Indian Country is jurisdiction. Since many reservations are on federal property, questions arise about who exercises jurisdiction over a particular crime. Is the FBI, Drug Enforcement Agency (DEA), Alcohol, Tobacco, and Firearms (ATF), Tribal Police, Bureau of Indian Affairs Police, County Sheriff, or City Police in charge? Depending on the crime committed, the area where it was committed, the race of the defendant, or the priorities of the prosecutor, any of these agencies or a combination of them may claim or reject jurisdiction.[21] Justice in Indian Country is in a confusing flux, often referred to as "the checkerboard problem." The challenge is to create workable, Indian-nation-specific policing and justice institutions that are infused with local, traditional custom.[22]

Beliefs about Justice

Notions of justice vary according to tribe, but are generally similar.

- Navajo spirituality encourages the restoration of harmony after a crime. A person who commits a crime has chosen to dishonor the worth of another person or his or her property. The community is likely to grieve communally for the fact that the perpetrator is less than he/she should be. Mediation is a common tool for dealing with harm caused. Victims and offenders might engage in a system of bartering to compensate for the loss.

- Lakota spirituality teaches that a victim should "let go" when he/she is harmed. Because of their aversion to materialism, they may tend to downplay the seriousness of property offenses. The harmful behavior and the weakness of the offender are the problems. The offender has to take responsibility for the harm caused, and is expected to restore the victim's loss. The community feels compassion for the victim and cares for the victim when he/she has been harmed.
  - The offender may be required to replace what was taken.

- The offender may be required to give away a personal possession in honor of the victim.

- In the case of a homicide, the offender may be required to take on the responsibilities that the deceased victim fulfilled in their family, such as providing financially for the surviving spouse and children.

Beliefs about Revenge

- Some tribes believe that justice should be left up to the Creator and, therefore, resist all forms of justice that do not seek harmony or try to restore balance.

- The offender is responsible for the crime, but revenge for honor is not a strong motivation among Native Americans.

- Offenders may be ostracized from the community or banished from the tribe for serious offenses if they do not find a way to demonstrate accountability for the harm caused.

Beliefs about Forgiveness

Forgiveness helps restore harmony and balance to the community.

- While Navajos have traditionally taken an attitude of disappointment toward the offender, they also have a strong sense of right and wrong. They understand that the offender has been unable to achieve his or her higher potential, and that the path previously chosen must change. More Navajos are now willing to consider the death penalty in cases where the offender expresses no remorse and indicates no willingness to change.

- Lakotas react similarly. They recognize the potential of criminal conduct in all humans and seek to balance concern for both the victim and offender with holding the offender accountable.

Reporting a Crime

Many Native Americans are distrustful of the American non-Native justice system, especially when they are required to deal with outsiders. They believe that the Federal and State justice systems favor non-Indians over Indians, and may conclude that their own police and courts are more fair to them.

- While unfamiliar with the criminal justice system and, therefore, unlikely to engage it, most Native Americans believe that society must be safe. Therefore, they generally are willing to cooperate with a criminal justice system to achieve that goal, even though they prefer their own system. They may need guidance in how to negotiate the Federal or State criminal justice system when they do report a crime.

- Most tribes place a high value on honesty, and Native Americans may be more likely than others to confess their guilt when confronted with an accusation. This may be one among several reasons that Native Americans are over-represented in the prison system.

Evidence Collection

As noted above, Native Americans may need guidance but are willing to participate in the criminal justice system if it is seen as a way of restoring balance and harmony to their community. Evidence collection is part of that process.

Family Reaction to a Crime

- Native American families grieve openly for victims. They do not assign blame to the victim or express shame that the victim has been harmed in an undignified way. The family and extended family support the victim, and the head of the family will often try to act on behalf of the victim.

- Since most Native Americans understand evil as "living out of harmony," the families regret that the offender was unable to meet the spiritual standards of harmony and balance in the community. They generally feel compassion for all involved.

- Tribal Councils and individual families may find it difficult to comprehend why federal victim/witness coordinators may offer services to the victim but not the offender, particularly in domestic violence cases.

- The role of alcoholism may be of concern to Native American families. Although highly variable among tribes, alcohol abuse is a factor in the five leading causes of death for American Indians (motor vehicle crashes, alcoholism, cirrhosis, suicide, and homicide). Among tribes with high rates of alcoholism, reports estimate that 75 percent of all vehicular crashes among American Indians are alcohol related.[23] Genetic, historical, cultural, and societal factors have contributed to this problem, and many Native Americans feel that it should be considered a mitigating factor in determining what is just.

Testifying in Court

- It is culturally appropriate for an elder in the family to speak on behalf of the victim when possible.

- Native American victims and offenders often appear in court with a dozen or so extended family members present to demonstrate support.

- When offered as an alternative to the mainstream adversarial criminal justice system in the United States, Native American families may prefer circle sentencing, family conferencing, or other more traditional and restorative justice practices.

Presenting Victim Impact Statements

- Native American victims will present victim impact statements in the criminal justice system.

- Immediate and extended family members may want to speak on the victim's behalf.

Restitution

- Native Americans generally feel that restitution, ordered to hold the offender directly responsible for the crime, may help restore essential balance to his or her life as well as help the victim.

- Many Native American victims may not be aware of crime victim compensation funds available on or off the reservations. Likewise, they may not know about special provisions and services for child victims under the Children's Justice Act and the Victim Assistance in Indian Country (VAIC) program. Victim/Witness Coordinators in the U.S. Attorneys' Offices should be able to assist these families, informing them of all available benefits and services, but should not become overbearing if families decline.

■ In many states, including New Mexico and Arizona, Native American medicine men and women may be paid for performing spiritual healing ceremonies by the State Crime Victim Compensation programs. Navajo medicine men and women sometimes seek the value of the cost of a sheep as payment for the ceremony.

Summary

■ While it is impossible to learn about all Native American Tribes or Nations, it is important to identify a spiritual advisor in each key tribe in the community. Death notifications should always be made to the head of the family (determine whether patriarchal or matriarchal) with a spiritual leader or elder from within the tribe.

■ Native American spirituality is not so much about events in historical time as it is about living with respect for the land, living in harmony within a specific community, and honoring spiritual leaders who have special healing powers within the community.

■ Organ donation and autopsy will be difficult for many Native Americans who do not want the body cut.

■ Burials usually take place four days after a death.

■ Most Native Americans believe that the spirit of a person lived before this life, during this life, and continues after this life. Spiritual communication with ancestors is common.

■ Many Native Americans do not trust the U.S. Justice system to be fair to them and prefer that misconduct be handled by one of the 175 Tribal Courts in the U.S.

■ Native American spiritual understanding of justice encourages restoration of harmony with attention paid to the victim, the offender, and the community. Thus, restorative justice principles are preferable.

■ Long silences are considered sacred time to many Native Americans. Most listen well and will respect your doing the same.

Things I Want To Remember From This Chapter

3
Hinduism

This brief description of Hinduism is not intended to be exhaustive. The authors recognize that within each faith there are divergent viewpoints. While we respect each individual's beliefs, it is impossible to represent all viewpoints in this limited forum. Therefore, the following information should serve only as a starting point for engaging Hindu clients or patients.

Like Native Americans, Hindus believe that theirs is the oldest religion. Hindu scholars have traced its roots back 6,000 to 8,000 years to the advanced Indus Valley civilization, but most Hindus believe that Hinduism was not originated by human beings. They say it had no beginning and it will have no end.

Hindus from around the world travel to the sacred waters and holy sites of India, the roots of their faith, for pilgrimage and to seek out religious teachers. *Hinduism* derives from the ancient linguistic root "to flow." Thus, rivers remain a central feature in Hindu religious life. In contemporary usage Hinduism is also sometimes referred to as *Sanātana Dharma*, a Sanskrit phrase meaning "eternal law."

Hindus compose one-sixth of the human family, more than 1 billion people. Hinduism is the root religion that leads to other similar faiths such as Buddhism, Sikhism and Jainism, as well as to a multitude of sects within Hinduism itself. Hindus are very tolerant of the views of others, emphasizing personal spiritual effort and experience more than moral rules or community religious practice. Hindus believe that God is everywhere. Therefore, no aspect of life is distinct from religion. Truth lies within human beings themselves.

In the context of world thought, Hinduism is a religion of the East. There is a vast difference between the ways seekers in the East and in the West tend to view ultimate questions such as "Who am I?" "Where did I come from?" and "Where am I going?" Whereas inner, personal experience is the crux of religion from the Eastern view, belief, and external religious practice tend to be valued more in the West. Eastern religions are accommodating of other views, believing that all paths lead ultimately to God.

Hindus believe that the soul slowly evolves through cycles of birth, death and rebirth to eventual enlightenment and liberation as the Self becomes fully realized. This process slowly frees human beings from the bondage of ignorance and desire. This eventual Truth, *moksha,* will leave none to suffer human frailties and faults. Hindus believe that there is no eternal hell, no damnation. All is good. All is God. Not one soul will be eternally deprived of its divine destiny of reunification with God.

Basic Beliefs and Rituals

Supreme Being

- Hindus worship one Supreme Divinity who is called by different names. This is because the peoples of India, with their different languages and cultures, have understood this Supreme Being differently.

- Hindus believe God is the eternal, ever-present source of all reality, omniscient and omnipresent, both imminent and transcendent.

- Hinduism has four principal denominations: Saivism worships God as *Siva*; Shaktism worships God as the Goddess *Shakti*; Vaishnavism worships God as Lord *Vishnu*; and Smartism, the most liberal denomination, leaves the choice of Deity up to the devotee.

- In addition to the Supreme Being, other gods are honored, most commonly Ganesha, Kartikkeya, Hanuman, and Ram. The Goddess of Divinity has multiple names including Durga, Parvati, Lakshmi, Kali, Saraswati, Sita, and Radha.

- God is worshipped through temple and home rites, devotional singing, and silent contemplation in meditation.

Images and Symbols

- Hindus use images and symbols of the divine in their worship.

- Most Hindu deities have human attributes, with the exception of a few who are depicted in animal form. Two of these, central to Hinduism, are included in most aspects of Hindu worship. The first is *Hanuman*, a monkey-faced deity who represents steadfast devotion. Worship of him is integral to learning devotion to the other deities. The other is the elephant-headed *Ganesh* or *Ganesha*. He is lord of auspiciousness, the sense of being surrounded by favorable circumstances. Ganesha is sometimes called the "Lord of Obstacles," referring to his influence over the karmas of life. He is the guardian of openings, travel, and new beginnings. He bestows blessings on worshippers as they enter the temple or start a new project.

- The *swastika* is an ancient religious symbol that signifies wellness, auspiciousness, and long life. Unfortunately, this mark of goodness was seized and perverted by the German Nazis.

- Hindus wear sectarian marks called *tilaka,* distinctive to their heritage, on their foreheads. A red, white, or beige dot on the forehead generally designates a practicing Hindu. Three parallel horizontal lines on the forehead, and often on the arms and chest, are made with an earthen paint or ashes and symbolize devotion to Shiva. Two or three vertical lines on the forehead identify one as being a devotee of one of the Vaishnav forms of the divine, especially Ram or Krishna. Traditionally, a small red line in the part of a woman's hair reveals her to be married. In contemporary times, this often is replaced with a red dot on her forehead. This dot is also thought to signify Shiva's third eye, a symbol of wisdom and divine sight. A black mark placed on the face of young children is intended to ward off evil.

Scriptures/Sacred Texts

Hindus believe in the divinity of the *Veda,* an ancient collection of divinely inspired scriptures. These primordial hymns are believed to be God's word. Today, Hindus use a variety of common scriptures, each one tending to focus on devotion to a different deity. The most popular of these is the *Ramayana*. The *Bhagavad-Gita* also is a commonly used sacred text.

Basic or Core Beliefs

■ Hindus have no unified body of doctrine, although there are five general beliefs common to most schools of Hinduism. These include:

- supremacy of non-violence;
- law of karma;
- process of reincarnation until one gains wisdom and spiritual perfection;
- need for a guru; and
- the ultimate unity of all existence.

■ The first three fundamental beliefs are shared with most schools of Buddhism: non-violence, karma, and reincarnation or rebirth.

- *Non-violence* is a crucial component in a Hindu's religious life because violence is believed to result in the most negative karma. All creation is an expression of the Divine and is to be held in reverence.

- *Karma* is the universal law of cause and effect. Every thought, word, and deed, both positive and negative, influences one's personal karma. It is carried forward, affecting both this life and future reincarnations.

- *Reincarnation* or *Rebirth* refers to the cycles of birth, death, and rebirth until enlightenment or liberation is reached. The spirit reenters the flesh in order to resolve and purify each negative, individual karma until the spirit is liberated from this cycle. At liberation, the soul is freed from rebirth into another physical body and ultimately merges into God, as a river merges into the sea that was its source. Likewise, Hindus believe that the universe itself goes through endless cycles of creation and re-creation.

■ Traditional Hindus pray before sunrise, at noon, and in the evening, with the prayers offered facing the East if possible. The East is where the Sun, source of life, rises.

- Hindus use flower petals, water, honey, incense, sandalwood paste, milk, and ghee (clarified butter) as offerings to the deities. These offerings, often seen in temples and in Hindu homes, are regarded as the precious, sweet, and life-giving natural elements. They are offered to God as a symbol of offering the best one has to give.

Spiritual Leaders

- There are many teachers and gurus within the Hindu tradition. Hindus believe that a spiritually awakened master, or *satguru,* is essential for them to know God, as are personal discipline, good conduct, purification, pilgrimage, self-inquiry, and meditation. Most Hindus follow the teachings and practices given to them by their own spiritual teacher.

- Mahatma Gandhi, a renowned Hindu leader, was popularly known in the West for his political activism based on non-violence. He was assassinated on January 30, 1948.

- Today, the Dalai Lama, a Tibetan Buddhist monk who has lived in exile for about 50 years, is acknowledged throughout the world for his emphasis on peace and human rights. He received the Nobel Peace Prize in 1989.

- Most gurus are either monks or priests. Monks are generally distinguished by their clothing, with the colors indicating their stage on the monastic ladder of their sect. In monastic settings, uninitiated monks wear white or yellow robes. Swamis, who are initiated Hindu spiritual leaders, wear saffron-colored robes. There are more than 3 million swamis in the world.

- Priests and other high caste males generally wear a white thread across their left shoulder to symbolize their vows to follow dharma and perform certain spiritual disciplines every day.

- Most gurus, monks, and priests wear a set of beads called *mala,* used like a rosary to keep count of the sacred words or mantras they repeat each day. The beads are made of different types of wood or seeds, depending on the sect to which the individual belongs.

- Out of respect for their teachers, believers sometimes bathe the feet of the guru.
- Female Hindu goddesses are revered and most male gods have female companions. While not common, women can hold spiritual leadership positions in Hinduism.[1]

Sites of Worship

- Hindus worship both in special shrines in their homes and in temples.
- Hindus remove their shoes when entering a home or temple as a sign of cleanliness and respect. Visitors should do the same.
- Hindus bring their offerings to the deities to temples. Rituals are performed with awe-filled gestures. Bells, lotus flowers, brightly colored cloth, and flower garlands decorate the images within the temples.
- Many forms of yoga and meditation are considered acts of religious practice and ways to commune with God.

Worship Day(s) of the Week

- Every day of the week is sacred, since each one is a special day to one or more of the major deities.

Special Days/Dates/Anniversaries

- Hindus believe that all living things are sacred. Certain animals, including cows, monkeys, peacocks, and snakes, are given special status because of their connection with various forms of the divine. The cow is especially revered as a symbol of the earth, the ever-giving nourisher. Veneration of the cow instills in Hindus the virtues of gentleness, receptivity and connectedness with nature.
- Hindus follow a sacred lunar calendar. Special rituals are performed on the full moon, the new moon, and on the eleventh day after each, as well as during many other astrological configurations. These times are considered particularly auspicious or favorable. Many Hindus regularly consult Hindu astrologers, especially at important

junctures of life such as marriage.

- In late summer or early fall, Hindus offer special rituals and meals for the souls of the dead.

Prohibitions

- Hindus are conservative about public expression of emotion, including affection. A husband seldom hugs or touches his wife in public. Hindus prefer to be greeted with both hands held together in front of the chest. Women, especially, will be uncomfortable shaking hands.
- While many Hindus are strict vegetarians, others are vegetarians only for rituals and religious observances.
- Many Hindus avoid foods that are thought to stir passion such as garlic or onions.
- Because eating flesh foods requires violence to animals, eating them is believed by many Hindus to diminish spiritual consciousness.
- Orthodox Hindus avoid alcohol because they believe it causes negative moods.
- Hindus believe that dairy products, grains, fruits, and vegetables are healthy.
- Modern Hindus are more flexible in their diet than traditional Hindus. For example, they may eat some poultry and fish but still avoid beef and pork.

Death and Dying Issues

Because belief in reincarnation is crucial to Hinduism, death is typically understood as the transition that ends one life and moves toward another. As such, there is minimal attention to death as final. It simply represents the soul's continuing journey. Nonetheless, the death of a loved one is a time of great sadness and grief because of the loss of the physical body. In speaking of the loved one who died, it is compassionate to affirm that the soul is now freed of earthly limitations and sorrows as it continues its spiritual journey. The soul is eternal and undying.

Grieving Hindus often find solace in traditional practices and customs. For example, family members are encouraged to visit their local temple often during their transition back to normalcy. To worship in the temple, to take garlands and fruits to their favorite deity, to cry at God's feet and seek God's grace are believed to be a natural and effective way to face grief. Similarly, they are encouraged to meet with a holy man or woman to obtain blessings and spiritual advice. Hindus give great credence to the words of saints and sages.

Other cultural ways of dealing with these difficulties can be found through *ayurveda* and *jothisha*. Survivors may be encouraged to visit an ayurvedic doctor, who will examine them, assess the nature of their physical, emotional and mental well-being, and prescribe breathing techniques to calm the mind, diet to keep the body healthy, and lifestyle changes to bring a balance of the forces back to normal. Ayurvedic doctors' emphasis on natural healing without complex drugs is common to Hindus. Additionally, they may want to consult with a *jothish* (astrologer), who will help them understand their particular life pattern, perhaps giving them insights and understandings into the whys and wherefores of untimely deaths.

Death Notification

- If possible, notification should be made by another Hindu, ideally a monk, priest or other guru. If that is not possible, someone from the culture of the family is preferable.

Anatomical Donation

- Organ donations are discouraged and, in some sects, prohibited. The Hindu faith believes the karma of the deceased person accompanies the organs. Hence, the recipient would be influenced subtly by the bad or good karma attached to the organ received. Further, the continued presence of the organ in another body may make it more difficult for the soul of the deceased donor to let go of the attachment to the physical world.

Autopsy

- Autopsy can be difficult for Hindus to accept, and should only be done when legally required, and as quickly after death as possible. When a person dies, the family should be allowed to cremate the body very soon after the autopsy is complete. This will allow the soul to let go of any physical attachment and prepare for a new life.

Body Preparation

- Because Hindus prefer cremation, which encourages the soul or spirit to move on in preparation for its next incarnation, very little preparation is necessary. If the body is not burned, the spirit might dwell longer or may return to occupy the body.

- Care for the body includes bathing the body with pure water, clipping the hair and nails, placing a few basil leaves in the mouth, and for women in some Hindu communities, adding a piece of gold or precious stone to the body.

- Traditional Hindus wrap the body in a white, unbleached cotton cloth. In the United States, it is common to dress the body in a suit or sari.

Funeral Practices

- The eldest son or an elder male relative is responsible for performing a set of ancient rituals at the cremation and afterward.

- In India and other countries where it is allowed, the body is placed on a pile of wood. The ritual leader walks four times to the left around the pyre and pours ghee over the body while the family chants divine names. The body is then covered with more wood. This approximately 800-pound pile of wood, the *pyre,* is lit and burned in open air. In India, the ashes are then swept into the River Ganges.

- In the United States, mourners wear mostly white and gather at the home for a final viewing of their loved one before cremation, which commonly takes place within 24 hours in a funeral home.

- Female relatives traditionally conduct ritual lamenting and weeping for the deceased. In some Hindu communities, women gather for ritual songs and prayers at the home of the deceased. In other Hindu communities, only the immediate family gathers for the lamentation, and others do not enter the home until eight to thirteen days after the death and cremation.

- For eight days to a month, the family observes a period of mourning and ritual impurity. During this time, members of the immediate family remain together and do not leave their home. To close this period, the family traditionally partakes of a ritual meal called a *shraddha,* marking the end of the family's initial mourning period and acknowledging the journey of the departed soul.

- The family arranges a memorial service in the local temple to observe the death anniversary.

- Some Hindus offer special rituals and meals for the souls of the dead during late summer and early fall.

Burial Practices

- If they can afford it, many Hindus in the United States fly their loved one's ashes to India to be scattered into the River Ganges or some other sacred water source.

- Some sects perform earth burials, but the burial site usually is not marked so no one can find and exhume the body. Monks and other holy persons such as gurus generally are not cremated, although they may be, especially if they are married. Those who are buried are usually seated upright in the lotus posture in a square crypt surrounded by salt. In India, these bodies may be placed directly into a river with the hope that they will eventually reach the ocean.

Beliefs About the Afterlife

- After death, the relatives minister to and nourish the dead person's spirit for ten days to a year through various rituals, taking into consideration the individual's circumstances. If this is not done, it is believed the spirit will continue to travel as a restless and potentially troublesome spirit. These rituals are usually performed in September.

- Troublesome forces known as *bhutas* or *pretas* are the spirits of those who died violently, too young, or after betrothal but before marriage. Resentful and frustrated, they wander around harassing the living until appeased by special rituals.

- After a period of disembodiment, the soul is reincarnated into a new body. Each new life is seen as an opportunity for greater spiritual progress, eventually leading all souls (not only Hindus) to spiritual enlightenment. Hindus do not believe in hell or eternal damnation, although there is a belief in purgatory-like forms of existence where the spirit suffers the effects of bad karma. Criminal offenders would be expected to suffer for their hurtful acts, not punished by God but by their own conscience and soul. This suffering could be fully experienced in the transitional period between death and rebirth, but only if the transgression was moderate. Horrific crimes would create karmas so profound as to take one or more lives in the future to resolve.

Justice Issues

Hindu tradition teaches that the universe has evolved through four stages, beginning with one in which truth and goodness prevailed to the current one in which ignorance prevails. The present cosmic cycle, called the *kaliyuga,* is considered the stage of deepest darkness and difficulty. Thus, since hardship and evil are inevitable in our current existence, it is important to act in as righteous a manner as possible and not to make things worse than they are.

Beliefs About Justice

The concept of karma is key to a Hindu understanding of justice.

- Hindus believe that each individual must ultimately experience the good or bad karmic consequences of all thoughts, words, and actions.

- Hardships, injuries, and inequalities are typically understood to be the result of previously accrued karma.

- Hindus are cautioned not to become overly obsessed with trying to determine why things happen to one's self or others. Only the Supreme Being knows each individual's karma. It is important to recognize, therefore, that Hindus might not be interested in criminal or civil justice procedures.

- Caregivers need to remember that while the notion of accrued karma can seem troubling, injustice is always wrong in Hinduism. Hindus recognize that efforts must be made to hold wrongdoers accountable for their actions and the negative karma that they created by their acts. Karma is not a blind acceptance of fate or helplessness.

- Because of their belief in karma as self-created, Hindus do not blame God for the difficulties or tragedies of life.

Beliefs About Vengeance

- Harming anyone in thought, word, or deed is to be avoided if possible.

- Hindus believe "evil doers" will inevitably reap their own punishment.

- Seeking revenge adds negativity to one's own karma. However, helping to seek and secure justice is not seen as wrong, provided one's actions are not based on a desire for revenge.

Beliefs About Forgiveness

- Granting forgiveness, or *kshama*, helps one accrue good karma and diminish bad karma.

- Forgiveness in the face of great suffering is believed to be a sign of spiritual strength.

- As witnesses in the legal systems, Hindu victims of crime may diminish the extent or seriousness of a crime.

Reporting Crime

Truth and non-violence are the two "wheels of the chariot" that carry a Hindu to spiritual realization. It is important for Hindu family members of someone killed to tell the truth if a crime is committed, even if it places him or her in danger of retaliation. On the other hand, the intent of revealing the truth must be a desire to end the wrongdoing nonviolently, not to take revenge.

Evidence Collection

The same philosophy holds true for evidence collection. Hindus may willingly participate if motivated by intent to prevent further suffering.

Family Reactions to Crime

- Hindus may be less likely to question a crime than members of other faiths, and are more likely to accept it as part of the person's karmic plan.
- Hindus may attribute misfortune or injury to a past word, action, or deed by the individual in this life or a previous life.

Testifying in Court

Hindus will generally view testifying like reporting. While often minimizing details, they may willingly testify if the intent is to promote truth and stop evil rather than to seek revenge.

Presenting Victim Impact Statements

- Some Hindus may feel that presenting a victim impact statement is a component of positively working through victimization.
- On the other hand, some Hindus may conclude that their own bad karma brought on the victimization. This may lead to self-blame and depression, especially when their experience causes hardship to members of their family and/or friends. Hindus with either of these points of view may understate their victimization and its impact or severity. They would not write or speak compelling impact statements. Others may decline to prepare statements.

Restitution

Restitution can be a means of balancing karma. Therefore, most Hindus would support restitution as beneficial for both the victim and the offender.

Summary

- For Hindus, inner, introspective personal spirituality is more significant than external religious practice.

- Hindus value astrology.

- Hindus worship One Supreme Deity called by different names.

- Belief in *karma* and *reincarnation* guide much of the behavior and attitudes of Hindus.

- Hindus avoid eating meat, especially beef and pork. They revere the cow as a symbol of the Earth, the ever-giving source of nourishment, and do not believe in the killing of animals.

- Hindus are conservative about human touch, so wait for them to take the lead. A slight bow with the hands held together in prayer position is favored.

- Death notifications should be made by a Hindu priest or monk if possible.

- Hindus seek to cremate their dead before sunset; therefore, organ donation and autopsy are very difficult.

- Hindus may have little interest in the criminal justice system because they believe that the Supreme Being assures ultimate justice through karmic influence on reincarnations.

- Harming anyone in thought, word, or deed is avoided; therefore Hindu court testimony may be weak, and they may have difficulty with victim impact statements. They may be most likely to cooperate with the justice system if they believe doing so will prevent further violence.

Things I Want To Remember From This Chapter

4
Buddhism

This brief description of Buddhism is not intended to be exhaustive. The authors recognize that within each faith there are divergent viewpoints. While we respect each individual's beliefs, it is impossible to represent all viewpoints in this limited forum. Therefore, the following information should serve only as a starting point for engaging Buddhist clients or patients.

Buddhism emerged out of Hinduism in Northern India in the 6th century BC (Before the Christian Era) and spread throughout much of Asia over the next thousand years. Buddha, which means "awakened one," is a term used to describe a person who reaches a state of complete enlightenment and, thereby, achieves release from the cycle of rebirth. The first known Buddha was Siddhartha Gautama, who formulated the core teachings of the faith.

Popular legend depicts Gautama as a sheltered young prince in Nepal who slipped outside the palace walls one day and observed overwhelming poverty, disease, and misery. The Buddha was able to experience enlightenment when he understood the true nature of suffering and the steps human beings could take to eliminate it from their lives.

The Buddhist path draws practitioners away from self-involvement and guides them into a broader perspective of fellowship and community. Buddhists focus on the basic goodness of life and strive to promote openheartedness, kindness, and compassion. They believe that the cultivation of mindfulness and awareness through meditation reveals the "treasure" that exists within every human being.

Buddhism has evolved into a complex philosophy over the last 2500 years. Modern Buddhism can be divided into three organized traditions.

- The first tradition emerged two centuries after the first Buddha's death and is known as Theravada. Generally speaking, Buddhists from Burma, Sri Lanka, Laos, Cambodia and Thailand are Theravadans. Vipassana, also known as Insight Meditation, is a branch of Theravada practiced widely in America.

- Mahayana originated in India at the beginning of the Common Era and later spread to China, Japan, Viet Nam and Korea, reflecting the spiritual influences of Taoism and Confucianism in those countries. Immigrants from those countries are likely to practice sub-groups within Mahayana Buddhism including Zen Buddhism, Pure Land Buddhism, and Nirchiren Shu Buddhism.

- Vajrayana developed in India in the 8th century and spread to Tibet where it absorbed elements of Himalayan shamanism. Buddhists from India and Tibet generally practice Vajrayana Buddhism.

American Buddhists may practice any of the above-mentioned traditions.

Buddhism is practiced by about 350 million people worldwide. It has grown from 400,000 to more than one million adherents in the United States in the last decade, although as many as four million may engage in some Buddhist practices, mainly through immigration. The degree to which an immigrant Buddhist assimilates into American culture can vary significantly. When experiencing traumatic life events such as deaths in the family, they may return intuitively to their more traditional practices, which may feel more safe and familiar, or they may attempt to utilize strengths from both traditional and more modern perspectives.

Just as people speaking the same language may use the same words but mean different things, Buddhists of the three traditions deal with the same concepts but may apply them in different ways. A single Buddhist doctrine may have radically different meanings among different groups. These contradictions in terms may be confusing. A sensitive caregiver should try to be aware of the "language" of Buddhism and be sensitive to the fact that the terms will mean different things in different contexts. "The caregiver should try to understand enough of the concepts of Buddhism to know how to ask the right questions of the person being served. The really fluent caregiver will be able to develop a sense of the possibilities of a belief system to see how it can be used to help the client or patient."[1]

Basic Beliefs and Rituals

Supreme Being

- There is no supreme being in Buddhism equivalent to God in other faiths. The Buddha (Gautama) taught that human beings are the arbitrators of their own destiny, and no intermediary is necessary. Over the centuries, however, differing views of divinity have evolved. While some Buddhists reject any form of divinity, other followers believe in divinities to whom they pray for guidance and blessings.

- Modern Buddhism is a philosophy and a way of life, and frequently is practiced in combination with other faiths.

Images and Symbols

- The most revered symbol in Buddhism is an image of a Buddha, an enlightened man in a sitting, meditating, or standing posture whose hands are held in one of several mudra positions that convey aspects of wisdom. The Buddha represents enlightenment, fostering an attitude of a focused mind and devotion. In a Buddhist home or temple, the Buddha statue usually is found on an altar amidst offerings of incense, flowers, and burning candles.

- The Bodhi Tree is a tree under which Buddha sat when he attained enlightenment. The image of the tree has come to symbolize Buddha's presence.

- The mandala is a sacred circle design representing the universe and symbolizing wholeness. Colorful and complex Tibetan mandalas are meant to be experienced as representations of the spiritual journey. Practitioners use them as visual aids for meditation.

Scriptures/Sacred Texts

- Few lay people regularly read the sacred texts of Buddhism, known as the Buddhist Canons, but many are familiar with specific verses and stories that convey the principle teachings.

- All versions are derived from oral teachings attributed to Gautama

Buddha, but each of the traditions has developed its own set of Canons.

Basic or Core Beliefs

- Buddhists describe the person or soul as a stream of mental energy that interacts with the world in a constantly changing manner. Karma is attached to that stream of energy. When the physical body dies, karma determines the process of rebirth.

- The Buddhist notion of karma grows out of the Hindu concept of cause and effect, but modern Buddhists have a wide variety of beliefs about karma that do not correspond to Hindu beliefs. Traditional Asian Buddhists may be fatalistic about their karma, even though it is a concept that allows for persons to shape their present and future lives with positive actions. Buddhism, as it has developed in America, however, stresses the liberating potential of right action in the present moment. As such, with regard to karma, Buddhism can be seen as spirituality in transition that takes an enlightenment-based view of social justice, working towards the collective good. While taking stock of the past is important, modern Buddhists are encouraged to exercise wisdom and compassion in their current actions and choose thinking and behavior reflecting the greater good.

- Three significant Buddhist concepts, commonly referred to as the Three Jewels, are the Buddha, the Dharma, and the Sangha. Practitioners "take refuge" in the Three Jewels to show respect for the Buddha, to acknowledge the Dharma as the totality of Buddhist teachings, and to embrace their Sangha or gathering of Buddhists peers for the collective purpose of pursuing the Dharma.[2] The term sangha among traditional Asian Buddhists, however, refers only to Buddha's enlightened followers and members of the monastic orders.

- Some Buddhists consider the concept of rebirth symbolic and choose instead to focus on pursuing the path of the Buddha in this life.

- The Four Noble Truths:

- Suffering is an unavoidable part of life.

- Suffering grows out of craving and ignorance.

- Cessation of suffering is possible by letting go of craving.

- By following the Eight-Fold Path, suffering can be eliminated and ignorance can be overcome.

  ▲ The Eight-Fold Path describes how to eventually be liberated from the cycle of birth and rebirth by cultivating the right (1) attitude, (2) intention, (3) speech, (4) action, (5) livelihood, (6) effort, (7) mindfulness, and (8) concentration.

■ The Five Precepts are vows taken by practitioners to affirm life and live virtuously by abstaining from certain behaviors. These prohibitions include:

- Do not kill, but cultivate compassion.

- Do not steal, but cultivate generosity.

- Do not commit sexual misconduct, adultery, or sexual abuse, but cultivate contentment.

- Do not lie, but cultivate truth.

- Do not use alcohol and other drugs, but cultivate mental clarity.

Spiritual Leaders

■ Abbott is the head of a temple in both Zen and Theravadan Buddhism.

■ Reverend and priest are terms used similarly to their English translations.

■ Sunim is a Korean teacher of Zen Buddhism.

■ Roshi is a Japanese teacher of Zen Buddhism.

■ Sensei is a general Japanese term for any teacher, and is often used for a Buddhist teacher.

■ Ajaan is a teacher of Theravada from Thailand, Cambodia, or Laos.

■ Bhante is a Theravadan term similar to reverend.

- Bhikkhu is a Theravadan monk who has taken special vows to renunciate worldly pleasures and possessions.
- Lama is a Tibetan Buddhist monk.
- Rimpoche is a Tibetan Buddhist formally recognized as an incarnation of a previously known Tibetan Buddhist lama.
- Geshe is a Tibetan Buddhist monk who has attained a high level of scholastic achievement.

Monasticism

- Ordained Buddhist monks and nuns devote their lives to bringing harmony and peace to their communities. They strive to transform suffering into happiness, embody goodness and truthfulness, and promote mindful, compassionate living. Monks and nuns command great respect from the Buddhist lay communities.
- Shaving their heads and wearing monastic robes conveys the monk's or nun's respect for the Buddha, the Dharma, and the Sangha.
- Robes, made up of 3-5 layers of cloth that vary in color and style, communicate monastic status, country of origin, and tradition. For example:
  - Japanese Zen monks and nuns wear black robes with leggings and a flat rectangular bag around their neck.
  - Tibetan monks and nuns wear saffron under robes and burgundy outer robes.
  - Korean Zen monks and nuns wear pale grey under robes with brown outer robes.
  - Thai, Cambodian, Laotian Theravadan monks wear ochre robes while the nuns wear white.
  - Sri Lankan Theravadan monks and nuns wear bright orange robes.
- Protocols for addressing Buddhist monks and nuns vary greatly among the three traditions, from such acts of respect as the removal of shoes and bowing in front of spiritual leaders to complicated rules of etiquette on physical contact, financial donations, and chaperoned meetings. Outsiders are not expected to know protocol

and therefore, it is appreciated when they make inquiries before meeting with a monk or nun to avoid awkward situations.

Sites of Worship

- Buddhists meditate in a temple, monastery or church. All have public areas where visitors are welcome and these visitors should remove their shoes as a sign of respect.
- Zendo is a meditation hall for Zen Buddhists.

Worship Days(s) of the Week

- Practicing Buddhists meditate, recite verses, and pray on a daily basis, and may do so in a place of worship.
- It is also commonplace for Buddhists to create an altar in a quiet area of their homes for their daily practice. This altar may be adorned with images of the Buddha, flowers, incense, sweets, and candles.

Special Days/Dates/Anniversaries

- With the exception of Japanese Buddhist holidays that are observed on fixed days according to the Gregorian calendar, most Buddhist holidays are based on the lunar-solar calendar.
- Theravadan Buddhists celebrate Buddha Day on the full moon in May to commemorate the birth, enlightenment, and death of the Buddha.
- Mahayana Buddhists celebrate the birth, enlightenment and death of the Buddha separately in May, February, and March respectively, according to the lunar cycle.
- Buddhist New Year is celebrated by Theravadans on the first full moon day in April.

Prohibitions

- Because they believe they should not harm animal life, many Buddhists practice vegetarianism.

■ Buddhists strive to avoid thinking bad thoughts, divisive speech, swearing, whining, and gossiping.

Death and Dying Issues

Buddhists place significant emphasis on death and dying because of their belief in the cycles of rebirth. Death is not the end of life. To Buddhists, reincarnation is an intangible reality that they accept but may not fully understand.

Reincarnation may be like an uncontrolled whirlwind in which one is blown about like the autumn leaves, not knowing where he or she will be dropped. Gehlek Rimpoche quotes a story from one of the Buddha's chief disciples:

> Mahakatyayana was walking through a forest with a group of students. They came across a lake where a man, a woman, and their baby were eating a fish they had just caught. Their dog was barking and begging for food. On catching sight of them, Mahakatyayana stopped and burst out laughing. Everyone wanted to know why. He explained, "The baby the mother now holds to her breast was, in his previous life, the man her husband murdered for having assaulted her. The fish they are eating was the baby's grandfather and the dog begging for a piece of that fish was his grandfather's wife.[3]

Buddhists believe that a calm and focused state of mind at the moment of death is important in determining the quality of rebirth. When death is timely, and the life has been successful and happy, the surviving family can be cheerful, even celebratory, as they focus on positive support to the departed person as he/she prepares for rebirth. On the other hand, death caused by trauma or during anger is considered harmful for the next life. Violent death is believed to "close the spiritual eyes." Space pervades, and the spirit remains close to the body, causing grave concern about their loved one's journey toward rebirth. Buddhists will attempt to ameliorate this condition through special prayers and rituals to enable the spirit to detach from the body.

When a person is gravely ill or badly hurt and expected to die, the family places an image of the Buddha within eyesight of the dying person. Family members remind their loved one of the good he/she has done. They seek to relieve anger and agitation, and help the person to spiritually prepare for death. When possible, monks attend the dying person to offer support in maintaining a calm state of awareness and to chant so that the person is soothed and has a positive object on which to focus the mind. A presiding monk will encourage the dying person to maintain awareness of breath until the last breath, since the next breath he experiences will be the moment of rebirth into another human body.

Practicing Buddhists do not ingest drugs or alcohol because of their ability to cloud the clarity of the mind. Therefore, to address pain and discomfort, guided meditation would generally be preferable to the use of painkillers and medication, but the decision would fall with the dying person and his or her family.

Death Notification

- The notifier of choice will be a Buddhist monk, priest, or nun who speaks the same language and knows the customs of the survivors are important for appropriate death notification.

Anatomical Donation

- Some Buddhists fear that the removal of organs might interfere with the delicate process of transition to rebirth. In Japan, cutting the body within 24 hours after death is a serious taboo.
- On the other hand, many Buddhists living in America believe that offering part of one's body so that another may live and prosper will reap positive karma.[4]

Autopsy

Among the Buddhist traditions there are various considerations when it comes to autopsy, and Buddhist victims/survivors could be motivated by any of them.

- Some Buddhists fear that cutting the body for autopsy will interrupt the process of transition to rebirth.
- It is taboo in some Buddhist cultures to perform an autopsy on a highly revered monk or nun.
- A Buddhist family wants the body to remain intact, particularly

when they see no positive karmic benefit of autopsy to the departed soul.

- The immediate removal of the body as a piece of evidence interrupts the grieving process. This prevents family members from preparing the body and ensuring the body a safe and serene environment, which is believed to be important for a good rebirth.

Body Preparation

- Many Buddhist families want the body to remain undisturbed for several hours after the loved one has ceased to breathe. They prefer a Buddhist priest, monk, or nun to be present to perform prayers and rites before the body is removed.

- The traditions vary in the interpretation of "moment of death." Theravadan and Mahayana Buddhists believe cessation of breath is the moment of death, while Tibetan/Vajrayana Buddhists believe that it occurs around the time that the body loses it fluids several hours later.

- For reasons of tradition and their own grieving, Theravadan and Tibetan/Vajrayana Buddhist families will want to wash the body, dress the body, and keep it at home to watch over it until the funeral takes place three to five days later.

- However, Mahayana Buddhists generally remove the body to the crematorium as soon as the medical examiner has declared the person deceased, and conduct the funeral service a few days later with the ashes present.

- Buddhists vary in their thinking about the importance of access to the body after death. Immediate and extended prayer and the intercession of enlightened beings on behalf of the departed are believed to be more important for the passage of the soul to the next life than the family's access to the body.

- Tibetan Buddhists observe the practice of prayers and rituals throughout a 49-day period, after which the deceased person is reborn.

Funeral Practices

Funeral practices among Buddhists vary greatly according to tradition and family custom. The following are directions for funeral rites in certain Theravadan traditions:[5]

- Invite four Theravadan monks to chant prayers for the sick person when he or she is seriously ill and death is near. Crying and wailing are inappropriate in the presence of the departed, both before and after the death.

- Cleanse the body immediately and clothe it in neat, simple attire without adornments or jewelry.

- Lay the body in a modest casket adorned with flowers and wreathes. Place a photograph of the deceased before the closed casket.

- Place a piece of yellow cloth at the front door of the home to identify the correct house. Donate contributions of cash from visitors to charities.

- The family stands in respectful silence when the casket leaves the house on the day of the funeral, reflecting on the mortality of the human condition and radiating good wishes to the deceased.

- Invite four monks to the home on the day of the funeral to chant and to offer the five precepts to the family, after which they will lead or follow the hearse to the funeral site.

- Play solemn music during the funeral procession.

- Each monk should be offered a robe just before the coffin is pushed into the furnace. Offer a tray of requisites including a pillow, mat, oil lamp and razor blades to be taken back to the temple. These acts of merit are transferred to the deceased.

- If the funeral is in the morning, arrange a lunch for the monks.

- Distribute red thread and sweets to relatives and friends on the day of the funeral (This is a uniquely Chinese tradition). Distribute handkerchiefs to differentiate between the mourners and those who attend the funeral.

- On the 49th day after death, make a donation to the monks and transfer the merit to the deceased.

Burial Practices

- Buddhists generally prefer cremation to burial. If members of the family cremate the body, the bones and ashes may be placed in a columbarium so they may later be collected and thrown into a body of water. They also may be left for disposal at the crematorium.

- Ashes and bones of important spiritual masters, saved as relics, are believed to have magical powers.

- The traditional sky-burial in Tibet has become a symbol of contemporary Tibetan Buddhist identity under Chinese domination, reflecting their belief that the physical body is a temporary shell for the spirit. Bodies wrapped in cloth are taken to mountaintop "burial rocks" at dawn where they are solemnly cut into pieces and fed to vultures.

Beliefs About the Afterlife/the In-Between State

- Once the soul separates from the body, it assumes its own form and passes into an "in-between" state before the next rebirth.

- A 9th century text known as The Tibetan Book of the Dead describes in great detail the soul's 49-day journey to rebirth. During this period, called the bardo, Tibetan Buddhist families read from the text to guide their deceased loved one in the transition to a new life.[6]

- When a person has died under unsettling circumstances, as a result of a violent crime or in a state of agitation, fear, or anger, the period of bardo may be longer than 49 days before the soul reincarnates.

- Buddhist families from all traditions perform regular services in their home or at their temple on behalf of the deceased.

Justice Issues

A Buddhist's perspective on justice and justice systems is intrinsically tied to cultural orientation, country of origin, and religious tradition. The universal law of karma is a justice system to which all Buddhists ascribe. An individual's attitude about karma will determine his or her response to crime-related deaths and may dictate his or her willingness to interact with justice systems.

Buddhists believe that the universal law of karma rewards meritorious actions with present and future happiness in this life and subsequent lifetimes, and punishes evil deeds with greater suffering in the future.

While liberation from rebirth may be the ultimate goal, Buddhism offers guidance about how to live in this world. Participation in the criminal justice system is good for personal karma if the motivation is to prevent harmful actions in the future. The challenge facing Buddhist family members whose loved ones have died as a result of murder or other forms of homicide is to overcome their desire to end the karmic connection with the offender that is causing harm. Buddhists who understand these deaths within the context of their personal karma might end all contact with the offender to avoid perpetuating the negative karmic relationship. This attitude, however, could be perceived as selfish.

Beliefs About Justice

- Among Buddhists from Thailand, Cambodia, Sri Lanka, and Laos, karma and karmic relationships usually are viewed as personal. A criminal death is payment for the victim's previous wrongdoing. The individual who commits the crime is viewed as a "karmic debt collector."
- Buddhists from Korea, Vietnam, Japan, and Tibet tend to interpret criminal victimization in broader terms. They view victimization as a combination of collective and individual karma, along with conditions in the world that permit such actions to take place. For example, these Buddhists might believe that those who died in the September 11, 2001 attacks on America were innocent of personal wrongdoing but guilty of extremely negative collective karma based on their profession, living in American culture, or other group life circumstance.

Beliefs About Revenge

- Buddhists try not to be agents of revenge. Seeking retribution is bad for personal karma. Acts of vengeance for bringing dishonor to a family are common to some Asian cultures, particularly Chinese, as a holdover from their pre-Buddhist culture. From a Buddhist point of view, such actions are considered extremely negative and harmful to personal karma.

- Blame is considered a destructive force. Spiritual practices in Buddhism address anger and embitterment. Buddhists try to avoid anger because it will breed more anger.

- Buddhist practice is to acknowledge anger without acting upon it. The antidote to anger is patience and should be totally engaged, concentrated, and enthusiastic. Buddhists seek to find a way to weaken the energy of the anger. One Tibetan Buddhist practice is to stand and bounce lightly on the balls of the feet and breathe softly 3, 9, or 21 times, allowing the breath to take away the angry thoughts and cool the disturbing impulses.[7]

Beliefs About Forgiveness

- Buddhists are encouraged to reflect on all the karmic conditions that "allowed" a negative event to occur. Their goal is to recognize the "truth of what happened." They might seek to forgive others and themselves, understanding that both blame and self-blame are destructive forces.

- Asian Theravadans hold a forgiveness ceremony as soon as possible after a death to provide the living an opportunity to ask forgiveness and address any grievances the departed may have before he or she moves on to rebirth.

- In traditional Buddhist communities in Thailand, after a murderer is apprehended, the police take the individual to the temple to address the body of the deceased victim and ask for forgiveness. Even if the body has been disposed, the offender is expected to make a visit to the temple to perform a forgiveness rite. In the United States criminal justice system, this approach to forgiveness is impossible to manifest.

Reporting Crime

- Preventing further harm is a more powerful motivation to report a crime than is punishing the offender.

- Bringing an aggressor to justice after victimization is often a low priority for Buddhist survivors. After a homicide, they are more likely to focus on prayers and support for their departed loved one during his or her transition to rebirth than on justice. However, reporting as a means to seek crime victim compensation from the state is considered acceptable.

- Recent political refugees tend to deeply distrust law enforcement and justice systems. They also fear reprisals from the offender or the offender's family.

- On the other hand, Buddhists have a karmic responsibility to prevent future harmful acts. Unwillingness to participate in the justice process could be considered selfish and motivated by self-interest, particularly when failure to participate may mean that others might be harmed.

Family Reactions

Many Asian cultures traditionally downplay hardships. Instead, they emphasize the virtues of patience, equanimity, and endurance during difficult times. Caregivers may find Buddhists reticent to acknowledge the pain and suffering they experience.

Evidence Collection

- Submission of evidence to assist in the prosecution of a criminal death case could fall into the category of preventing future harm.

- Submitting evidence could be considered less personal than identifying an offender in a line-up. A Buddhist who has reservations about personally participating may be willing to present material evidence.

Testifying in Court

- Fear of reprisal, fear of the judge, and reluctance to harm their personal karma might be reasons Buddhists may not wish to testify in court.

- Before agreeing to testify, practicing Buddhists examine their motivations to be sure they are acting out of concern for the safety and well being of others and not out of revenge against the perpetrator.

Willingness to testify in court may be motivated by the desire to prevent further harm to the family and the community. Caregivers might motivate a Buddhist to testify in court by emphasizing the prevention of future harm.

Presenting Victim Impact Statements

- All of the above-mentioned factors that affect a Buddhist's willingness to participate in the criminal justice system are relevant with regard to victim impact statements.

- A cultural tendency among many Asian populations to minimize pain and suffering must be overcome before they can submit a compelling victim impact statement.

Restitution

- Fear that restitution will maintain an unwanted personal connection with a karmic debtor limits interest in its requisition.

- On the other hand, giving and receiving fair restitution for harm done is a means of cleansing the negative karma brought on by the crime.

- Holding a person accountable for harm through restitution is viewed as beneficial to the victim, the offender, and society.

- Therefore, the contradictory nature of the above attitudes should be taken into account when a caregiver attempts to help a victim consider restitution.

Summary

- A slight bow with hands held together is a respectful way to greet Buddhists.

- Like Hindus, Buddhists believe that enlightenment is eventually reached through reincarnations based on accrued karma.

- Buddhists believe that suffering is unavoidable and that it grows out of craving and ignorance. Learning to let go of cravings and desires reduces suffering and helps one move toward enlightenment.

- Buddhists practice non-violence and, therefore, many Buddhists avoid eating meat.

- Death notifications should be made by a Buddhist if possible.

- Organ donation and autopsy are problematic for some Buddhists who believe that disturbing the body disrupts the transition of the soul.

- Buddhists may be reluctant to participate in the justice system because their goal is to diminish negative feelings and accept what is. The adversarial nature of the justice system may be counter-productive to this goal.

- Buddhists may participate in the justice system if they believe they have a karmic responsibility to prevent further victimizations.

- Buddhists may be reluctant to present victim impact statements because it could create unwanted karmic connection with the offender. They may be most likely to present a statement if they believe that doing so cleanses some of the negative karma associated with the crime.

Things I Want To Remember From This Chapter

5
Judaism

This brief description of Judaism is not intended to be exhaustive. The authors recognize that within each faith there are divergent viewpoints. While we respect each individual's beliefs, it is impossible to represent all viewpoints in this limited forum. Therefore, the following information should serve only as a starting point for engaging Jewish clients or patients.

Judaism rejected earlier belief systems that focused on nature and multiple spirits. The key feature of Judaism is recognition of one God, a kind, personal God who created and continues to care for humankind.[1]

According to the Torah, the holiest literature of Judaism, Abraham was told by God to go forth to a land that he would be shown and from him, a great nation would be born. Abraham was old and did not know where he was going, but he went. He left Mesopotamia more than 3400 years ago, by conservative estimates, to eventually settle in Canaan; and from this point on Abraham and his one God establish an unbreakable bond. His descendants were later enslaved in Egypt and eventually led out of slavery by Moses. These "Children of Israel" traveled for 40 years before settling down in what is today Israel and Jordan. During these years, Moses received Jewish law, a compilation of rules and laws including the Ten Commandments, by divine revelation.[2]

In A.D. 66, the Jews, under control of Rome, staged a successful revolt, but the Romans returned, defeated them, and destroyed their Temple in A.D. 70. At this point the dispersion (Diaspora) of the Jews began, and they were scattered all over the ancient world with no place of their own.

In the late 19th century, a Viennese journalist named Theodor Herzl began a movement for the Jewish people to once again inhabit Palestine, which at that time was part of the Ottoman Empire. The State of Israel as it is known today was created in 1948 after World War II, but the Arab states being displaced immediately declared war, and there were subsequent wars in 1967 and 1973, which were won by Israel.

Although Israel was established as the Jewish homeland, the State of Israel has no official religion. In fact, more than half of the Jews in Israel are considered secular Jews, who rarely observe the Jewish faith.

There are about 13 million Jews in the world. In the United States, the number of people who consider themselves Jews according to Jewish law (one whose mother is Jewish or one who has converted to Judaism) has decreased from about 5.5 million a decade ago to about 5.3 million today, a phenomenon generally attributed to interfaith marriage. Conversely, however, the number of Jews affiliating with synagogues has increased 15% to about one million people.

There are currently four branches of Judaism: Orthodox, Reform, Conservative, and Reconstructionist. All branches believe in one God with no separate manifestations. Although the branches differ in rituals, the basics of their faith are the same. All of life is to honor the Creator. However, since religious practice varies widely among the branches, caregivers must not assume that all Jewish religious behavior is similar.

The Orthodox branch, which includes about 21 percent of Jews in the United States,[3] is the most literal in its interpretation of the scriptures. Its proponents are the most traditional in how they live and worship. Men and women are separated in the services and they propose strict adherence to dietary, clothing, personal appearance, and behavioral expectations. A subsystem within Orthodox Judaism is Hasidism, which is divided into several sects and most known for its mystical practices.

The Reform movement began in Germany when many Jews became convinced that orthodox practitioners were losing touch with rapidly changing societies and they, therefore, liberalized many orthodox practices to incorporate more modern culture. This movement took root in North America more than 130 years ago under the leadership of Rabbi Isaac Mayer Wise, one of several European rabbis who brought the European changes in Judaism to this country. Reform Judaism is now the largest Jewish movement in North

America and includes about 39% of Judaism, about 1.5 million people in more than 900 congregations.

Conservative Judaism is the second largest group, about 33 percent of all Jews in this country. Conservative Jews retain some traditional Jewish practices but believe that meaningful observance of Judaism continues to evolve.

The most recently formed group is the Reconstructionists, about three percent of the Jews in the United States. Reconstructionists view Judaism as an evolving religious civilization. They reject the idea of God as a personal sustainer as well as the understanding of Jews as "the chosen people." Based on the theology of Rabbi Mordecai Kaplan, they observe Jewish rituals and practices more for cultural than religious reasons.

In addition, a loose network of independent Jewish congregations forms a vibrant Jewish renewal movement in the United States that does not identify with any of the four organized branches of Judaism. Others may refer to themselves as secular humanist Jews who honor Jewish history and culture but do not believe in God.

Basic Beliefs and Rituals

Supreme Being

Jews believe in monotheism. There is only one God, commonly referred to as Adonai, or Yahweh. Orthodox Jews are very careful to fulfill the commandment not to take the name of God in vain. Therefore, even in writing, they use the word "G_d" rather than "God" and Y_H_V_H rather than "Yahweh."

Images and Symbols

- Jews do not use figures or statues in rituals, believing these to be "graven images" prohibited by Scripture.
- The Star of David, generally representing Judaism, is composed of two equilateral triangles forming a hexagram. The triangle pointing downward represents God's interest in, love for, and expectations for humanity. The triangle pointing upward represents the human

being's obligation to love, yearn for, and obey God. Judaism balances these two forces through its system of mitzvot or commandments. There are 613 mitzvot in the Torah. Jewish law describes how the 613 mitzvot commandments are to be observed. The Star of David was an identifying badge used by the Nazis for Jews and is now the central image on the flag of Israel.

- The Menorah, a seven-branched candelabrum, is a symbol of the nation of Israel that represents its mission to be "a light unto the nations." The Chanukia is a nine-branched candelabrum used during Chanukah (or Hanukkah), usually in December, which means "dedication." One additional candle is lit each night for eight days in remembrance of how a one-day supply of oil lasted for eight days during the Maccabean revolt when the Temple was rededicated after its defilement by the Syrian-Greek king, Antiochus IV.

- Jewish practitioners wear symbolic clothing, such as the yarmulke or kippah, a skullcap worn by men and occasionally by women in Conservative and Reform religious services, which represents humility before God. Some Orthodox and Conservative men wear their yarmulkes at all times, sometimes under a plain black Fedora or Homburg hat when they are outside.

- Prayer shawls (Tallits) remind Jews of the presence of God and include outer fringes representing Jewish laws.

- Some Orthodox men wear long black overcoats and cotton or wool under- garments with knotted corner fringes to remind them of the Commandments of God.

- Some Jews wear phylacteries ("tefilin"), which are small, black leather boxes containing texts of Scripture, for morning prayer.

- Some Jewish homes have a mezuzah attached to the doorway, which is a small box containing a parchment with four chapters from the Torah written on it. These chapters contain the fundamental, defining truths of Judaism. Some religious Jews, as they enter or leave, stop to meditate about these truths and then kiss the mezuzah as an expression of love and affirmation for God and the Torah.

- Symbolic hairstyles among orthodox Jews include the growth of side locks where men and boys do not cut their forelocks in response to the Biblical command to "not trim the hair on your temples."

Scriptures/Sacred Texts

- Primary scripture for Jews is the Torah, the first five Books of what Christians call the Old Testament, which begins with creation of the world and ends with the death of Moses. The Torahs in temples and synagogues are hand-written on scrolls of parchment and kept in special cabinets called arks. They are also published in book form in Hebrew and many other languages.

- Additional honored scriptures include the Prophets or Niviem (the stories of Joshua, Isaiah, and Jonah) and the Writings or Kituvim (Psalms and Proverbs). These 24 books (Torah, Prophets, and Writings) make up the Hebrew Bible or Tanakh.

- The Talmud is a multi-volume treatise of commentary on the Torah and expansion of Jewish law. The Talmud also includes stories that reflect culture and traditional knowledge to help Jews interpret the Torah.

Basic or Core Beliefs

- Jews believe that God spoke directly to the patriarchs Abraham, Isaac, and Jacob, and revealed the Torah (including the Ten Commandments) to Moses for the Jewish nation at Mount Sinai.

- Jews believe God is just and expects humankind to act justly and ethically. When individuals act in contrast to goodness, they sin and are required to seek forgiveness from both the persons sinned against and from God.

- Judaism provides a detailed code of conduct to ensure the survival of this ancient people. Believers are tied to the land of Israel and the cultural heritage of their ancestors. Jews generally do not employ missionaries or seek converts, believing that all moral, righteous people have a share in the afterlife. (However, Lubavitchers are a subgroup of about 25,000 Hasidic Jews who live near their Brooklyn headquarters and are dedicated to evangelizing other Jews whose faith is less radical. They hope to bring all secular and liberal Jews "back into the fold."

- Conversion from other faiths is discouraged but is possible. Intermarriage and the decrease of the Jewish population are of major concern; therefore, Jews are strongly encouraged to marry other Jews.

- Traditionally, Jews have believed that a Messiah, a direct descendant of King David, would remove evil from the world and establish peace. A more modern view, generally expressed in Reform Judaism, is that a Messianic Age will eventually be accomplished on earth when all people choose to live in peaceful relationship.

Spiritual Leaders

- Rabbis (teachers) are the spiritual leaders of Judaism. In the more liberal branches, both men and women can be rabbis. Rabbis are permitted to marry in all branches. Any knowledgeable Jew over the age of 13 may conduct worship (males only in Orthodox congregations).
- Cantors are worship leaders who sing and lead the congregation in liturgical music during the services.

Sites of Worship

- The synagogue (also referred to as shul) or temple is the primary house of worship where both group and individual prayers are offered. At the front of the synagogue or temple is the bimah or platform, where the ark is located and where the Rabbi speaks.
- Public worship is conducted as long as ten or more adult male Jews over the age of Bar Mitzvah come together for the purpose of communal prayer (minyan). Women are also considered as part of the minyan in most Reform synagogues and prayer gatherings.
- Hebrew is the sacred language of Judaism, but the degree of its use varies among the branches. Orthodox services are nearly always in Hebrew.
- All synagogues have a continuously burning sanctuary lamp above the Ark (Eternal Light) to symbolize God's presence and to recall the continually burning lamp in the Jerusalem temple.
- In Orthodox services, the genders are separated by a partition.

Worship Days(s) of the Week

- Traditional Jews worship daily in the morning and evening.

- The Shabbat, or Sabbath, begins at sunset on Friday night and is intended for rest, reflection, and study after six days of work. The Sabbath lasts until nightfall on Saturday. Both Friday night and Saturday morning services are held. Orthodox Jews do not work (including writing, using a vehicle, handling money, turning electrical devices on and off, etc.) during this time. To honor Jewish tradition, it is important not to schedule activities on Friday afternoons, especially during the winter when sunset comes early, or Saturday.

- An important part of Friday night activities includes the gathering of family members for prayer, candle lighting to symbolize joy, and dinner. This historic tradition symbolizes the religious observances continued by Israelite families when their ancient temples were destroyed. It also honors the sanctity and dignity of human life, which is like God's close and covenantal relationship with Israel.

- Some synagogues hold services three times per day, each day of the week; some offer Hebrew School on Sundays, after the Sabbath.

Special Days/Dates/Anniversaries

- Rosh Hashanah is the Jewish New Year, a two-day holiday which comes in September or October, depending on the lunar calendar. Rosh Hashana initiates a ten-day period, the Ten Days of Repentance, which culminates in Yom Kippur. During these days, Jewish people make an accounting of how they have cared for the creation that God has entrusted to them and how they have carried out their moral responsibilities during the past year. It is a period when they place additional focus on living as God intended for them to live.

- Yom Kippur is the Day of Atonement. On this one-day holiday, Jews fast, foregoing food and drink. They do not work, but devote the day to repenting for their misdeeds during the past year and asking forgiveness from those they have wronged or harmed. They gain atonement from God for their sins after seeking forgiveness from people they have wronged.

- Passover (Pesach) is a major eight-day holiday in the spring in which the delivery of the Jewish people from slavery in Egypt is celebrated. Jews give thanks that Jewish males were spared or "passed over" from death. The Passover activities include feasts on the first two nights of the holiday called Seder, where foods symbolic of the slavery and redemption are eaten as the Exodus story is paraphrased and folk songs are sung. Observant Jews limit themselves to a very strict, distinctive diet during the entire Passover holiday, especially the exclusion of all foods made with leaven (breads, cookies, cakes) and certain grains.

- Other significant rituals include the brit milah on the 8th day after birth when male babies are circumcised, the bar mitzvah for males, and the bat mitzvah for females when they reach adolescence, generally the 13th year when they are ready to assume full membership into the community. These later rituals require considerable study and demonstration of competence in Jewish beliefs and practices.

- Chanukah (Hanukkah) is an eight-day celebration of a second-century BCE war victory over Syria for religious independence. It usually falls in December and is also is called the Festival of Lights. One more candle is lit each night of the eight days to celebrate the fact that when the Jews again gained possession of the Temple, the lamp burned for eight days on one day's supply of oil. Chanukah is actually a minor Jewish holiday but it has been emphasized in predominantly Christian countries because it occurs around Christmas time, providing Jewish children the opportunity to enjoy the secular aspects of the holidays similarly to Christian children.

- Other Biblical holidays include Succot/Simchat Torah, a harvest festival in the fall when the last chapters of the Torah are read and the yearly cycle of reading the Torah again is begun; Purim, a festival in late February or early March when Esther's rescue of the Jews of ancient Persia is remembered; and Shavuot, a spring celebration when the revelation of the Torah to Moses on Mt. Sinai, including the Ten Commandments, is remembered.

- The 20th century brought the inclusion of two additional

commemorations: Yom HaShoah, Holocaust Memorial Day, and Yom Ha'Ats'ma'ut, Israel Independence Day.

- Orthodox Jews observe the Biblically-mandated holidays in much the same way as they observe the Sabbath (see below). Purim, Chanukah, Yom HaShoah, and Yom Ha'Ats'ma'ut do not have these restrictions.

Prohibitions

- Jews believe that Sabbath rest means limited or no work or physical labor. Orthodox Jews interpret Sabbath laws strictly by also refraining from driving, writing, or use of electricity from sunset on Friday to nightfall on Saturday.

- Orthodox and some other Jews adhere to kosher dietary laws. Described in the Hebrew Bible and further expanded in the Talmud, kosher dietary restrictions refer to foods prepared according to Jewish ritual standards. Most Jews do not eat pork. To be kosher, poultry and meat from animals that chew a cud and have cloven hoofs (such as cows and sheep) must be slaughtered in accordance with specific procedures that include removing all traces of blood. Seafood is considered kosher if the fish have scales or fins (not shellfish). Kosher meal preparation requires separate cooking and serving utensils for dairy products and for meat products. Dietary guidelines prohibit consuming dairy products at the same time as meat products.

- Judaism highly values modesty in behavior, speech, and dress for both men and women. Many Orthodox Jewish men and women do not touch members of the opposite sex outside of their families. They do not initiate a handshake with a member of the opposite sex, but may respond to an outstretched hand in order not to embarrass anyone.

Death and Dying Issues

Simplicity, dignity, and equality govern treatment of the dead, burial, and mourning rites of Jewish people. The dynamics of Jewish custom are designed to help the mourner accept the reality of death's finality, as far as earthly existence is concerned, and to help the mourner gradually return to the tasks of life. Judaism includes a range of beliefs from no view of the afterlife to belief in the resurrection of the body and the immortality of the soul.

Death Notification

If possible, a rabbi or representative of the Jewish faith should notify the family of the death.

Anatomical Donation

- Some traditional Jewish authorities oppose organ donation because it fails to honor the natural decomposition of the body with all body parts intact.
- Others do not see organ donation to save, prolong, or enhance the life of a sick person as a desecration of the body. Jewish law does not allow donation for theoretical research or educational purposes.

Autopsy

- An autopsy will not likely be allowed unless it is crucial from a legal perspective. Autopsies violate the Jewish mandate forbidding mutilation of a dead body.
- When an autopsy is required, Jewish tradition requires that all body parts be placed back in the body.

Body Preparation

- Jewish treatment of the body emphasizes reality, simplicity, and respect for the body as created in God's image. Judaism traditionally opposes cremation, especially after the Holocaust, as failure to honor the natural decomposition of the body.
- Embalming is similarly rejected, although it is becoming more common in Reform Judaism. In traditional Judaism, the body is taken to the funeral home where two or three persons of the same gender from the congregation cleanse and bathe the body. This ritual is called tahara. All adornment, such as dentures or nail polish, is removed so that the body leaves the world as purely as it

entered it. The body is dressed in a white, seamless, linen or muslin shroud including a shirt, pants, belt, and hood-like covering, the front of which resembles a veil.

- The body is placed in a wooden coffin that is then closed. Plain coffins are deemed appropriate.
- Visitation before burial is not encouraged because grief is so poignant. Attending to visitors may seem like a burden.

Funeral Practices

- The body is not left unattended from the time of death until it is buried, generally within 24-48 hours. A candle is kept lit beside the body to symbolize the soul of the deceased.
- Attending to the dead is considered one of the purest Jewish rituals because there is no reciprocity.
- Most deceased Conservative and Reform Jews are dressed in ordinary clothing. Some wear prayer shawls and yarmulkes.
- The bodies of some Reform Jews are embalmed and prepared similarly to Christians. The body is placed in a plain wooden coffin, which is closed.
- Traditional Judaism does not support public viewing of the deceased, but liberal Judaism allows viewing by immediate family members who may benefit psychologically.

Burial Practices

- Following the funeral, the body is taken to the cemetery where it is buried in the ground. Mourners shovel earth onto the grave as their last respectful act for the deceased. They often do this with the back of their shovels to indicate their reluctance to perform the ritual.
- Any violation of the body that interferes with the performance of these rituals causes distress. When a loved one's body is not recovered after death, such as following the Oklahoma City Murrah Building disaster or the September 11 tragedy, Jewish people suffer significant emotional and spiritual pain because of the desecration

of the body. For example, after the 9/11 murders, Jewish students in New York City kept prayerful watch over the truck loads of body parts collected because they assumed that some of the victims were Jewish. It is important to Jews that remains of victims of violence be collected so they can be buried.

- Shiva is the seven-day mourning period (excluding the Sabbath which is always a day of joy) during which work is avoided and mourners are assisted in their daily needs by others. Immediate family members of the deceased may wear a torn piece of clothing or a torn black ribbon as a symbol of humility and mourning. Mirrors are covered in the home and family members may sit in low chairs indicating humility before God.

- At the time of death, at the funeral, and each day for a year, the mourner's prayer, the kaddish, is prayed. This prayer is one of adoration of God without mention of death. The kaddish is prayed at worship services to remember those whose death anniversaries occur that week.

- Sheloshim is the remaining 23 days of the month when mourners return to their normal routine but avoid celebrations. Community support is crucial during these phases.

- Flowers are generally not part of Jewish funerals or mourning periods. Most Jews consider a donation to a worthwhile charity more appropriate.

- Avelut is the year following death. During this time, a headstone is unveiled, mourning generally is concluded, and focus returns to living. Visitors to the grave often lay small stones on the headstone to show they have visited.

- The names of the deceased are often recorded on the memorial board in the synagogue and are remembered every year on the anniversary of their death (jahrzeit).

Beliefs About the Afterlife

- Jewish people focus on leading a good life in this world, understanding that proper behavior in this world is the only way to prepare for the afterlife. Since God is seen as ultimately just, injustices on earth are believed by traditional Jews to be dealt with in the afterlife as a way to reflect ultimate justice.

- Gehennom has been identified as a place where souls may be punished. However, since Jews understand God to be filled with mercy and love, punishment is not eternal.

- Jews believe that one's position in the afterlife, defined by lesser or greater closeness to God, is a function of the amount of good that a person did in this world.

- Some Jews believe that punishment might be self-determined on the basis of any suffering the person brought about to others.

Justice Issues

For Jews, the purpose of law must be to promote human life. Since God made a covenant with Abraham to care for the Jewish people, they, likewise, are to care for other human beings. The Talmud proclaims that it is greater to serve one's fellow man than to preoccupy oneself with divine communication. There is no higher priority than saving a life. A commonly quoted Talmudic statement is "He who saves a single life; it is as if he has saved the entire world."

Beliefs About Justice

- Jews face evil in the world with the hope that good eventually will prevail over evil as the faithful imitate God and enter into partnership with Him to repair and perfect Creation.

- Jews believe God is ultimately just and, likewise, expects humankind to act justly and ethically because humans are created in God's image.

- Jews believe those who hurt others must repent and change their ways or expect to be dealt with justly by God and humankind.

- Applying Jewish ethical values to current situations is of paramount importance. What is deemed ethical is determined by careful consideration of past and present teachings and situations.

- A beit din is a formal court of law within Orthodox Judaism that includes case law, standards of evidence, testimony of witnesses, etc. Orthodox Jews with civil concerns may wish to approach theses courts to help them resolve differences.

Beliefs About Revenge

- Justice tempered with mercy will result in overcoming evil.
- Jews believe that God may choose to forgive the offending person when that person has repented and attempted to make amends for the harm caused. Forgiveness is not the unilateral responsibility of the person harmed.
- Revenge, in sharp contrast to justice, is forbidden.

Beliefs About Forgiveness

- When individuals act contrary to goodness, they are required to seek forgiveness.
- Jews seek forgiveness from people for sins against people and from God for sins against God (which includes sins against people).
- Jews believe in six aspects of repentance: acknowledgment of the wrongdoing, remorse, apology, restitution, reconciliation, and resolution to never again repeat the inappropriate behavior.
- A Jew is not required to forgive unless the wrongdoer asks for forgiveness. There is no proactive requirement for someone harmed to forgive. Forgiveness rests on the shoulders of the offender. Asking forgiveness without attempting to undo the damage done and the pain inflicted is hollow. Since someone killed is not capable of forgiving, the wrongdoer cannot acquire forgiveness from someone else on the victim's behalf. Only after an offending person has done everything he or she can to undo the wrongdoing and asks for forgiveness is a response from the harmed person required. Genuine requests for forgiveness are to be taken seriously and responded to affirmatively. If the person harmed is reluctant or emotionally unable to forgive, the offender must make two more sincere attempts to apologize and reconcile. After three times, the offending person is not required to attempt again.

Reporting Crime

- Jews are obligated to speak out when others are in danger.
- Jews understand that willfully striking a human being is akin to striking an image of God.
- Jewish law abhors and condemns family violence. The Talmud states, "A man must never create an atmosphere of fear or violence in his household."

Evidence Collection

Jews support the collection of evidence in the course of seeking justice.

Family Reactions to Crime

Judaism forbids a person to strike another person willfully and maliciously. The Talmud states, "Raising one's hand as if to strike (i.e., before one has struck, or to create the impression that one is about to strike) is sufficient to earn one the title and status of a wicked person." Therefore, Judaism condemns even threatening to harm another person.

Testifying in Court

Jews are generally willing to testify in court. Some will prefer to "affirm" rather than "swear," since oath-taking and invoking God's name are serious awe-inspiring activities. Since traditional Jews will not swear or affirm on a Christian Bible, a Tanakh or Hebrew Bible should be available for Jewish witnesses.

Presenting Victim Impact Statements

Jewish victims will generally have no qualms about speaking about the impact of crime perpetrated on themselves or family members.

Restitution

In contrast to some Christian positions that forgiveness is required even without repentance, Jewish people require the offender to be aware of the wrongdoing, express remorse, and make reparations.

Summary

- The Jewish Sabbath is from sundown Friday until sundown Saturday, which should be taken into consideration in scheduling events.

- Orthodox and Conservative Jews will not eat pork or shellfish, and will require that food be kosher.

- Modesty is valued by Jews, and Orthodox Jews may be hesitant to touch members of the opposite sex. Wait for them to initiate a handshake.

- Death notifications should be given by a Rabbi, if possible.

- Jews believe that humans were made in the image of God and therefore avoid any violation to the body after death, including autopsy and embalming. They favor natural decomposition of the body and seek burial as soon as possible. They do recognize the need for autopsy in criminal cases as a means of seeking justice.

- Jews have few qualms about participating in the justice system.

- Jews believe that God is just and expects human beings to likewise seek justice. They are reluctant to forgive unless an offender has recognized his or her sin, felt remorse, repented, sought to make restitution to the victim, and reformed his or her behavior.

- Invoking an oath, or swearing, in God's name is taken very seriously by Jews and traditional Jews will not be comfortable being sworn in court on a Christian Bible. A Hebrew Bible should be available in courtrooms.

Things I Want To Remember From This Chapter

6
Christianity

This brief description of Christianity is not intended to be exhaustive. The authors recognize that within each faith, there are divergent viewpoints. While we respect each individual's beliefs, it is impossible to represent all viewpoints in this limited forum. Therefore, the following information should serve only as a starting point for engaging Christian clients or patients.

Christians honor their roots within Judaism but believe that Jesus, who lived on earth more than 2,000 years ago, revealed God as compassionate toward all humanity. For Christians, Jesus was the Messiah for whom the Jews had been waiting.

There are more than two billion Christians in the world. In the United States, 76.5 percent of the adult population claims to be Christian, an increase of 5 percent since 1990.[1] Numbering more than 150 million in the United States, Christians practice in more than 2,000 different denominations or groups.[2] About 88 million are Protestants, and about 62 million are Catholics. A much smaller number are Eastern Orthodox Christians, primarily Greek Orthodox and Russian Orthodox, with the national designations reflecting cultural traditions of each group's members. The organization *Christian Churches Together (CCT)*, a broadly based, inclusive, Christian ecumenical movement, identifies five categories of Christians: Evangelical/Pentecostal, Historic Protestant, Historic Racial/Ethnic, Eastern Orthodox, and Roman Catholic.

"The Handbook of Denominations in the United States identifies and describes 31 Baptist groups or conventions in the United States, the largest being southern Baptists, who now number 16.3 million."[3] The largest predominantly African American denomination, with more than eight million members, is the National Baptist Convention, U.S.A.[4] Most Christian congregations are small, with only 10 percent having more than 350 regular participants, according to the National Congregations Study.[5]

While Catholicism continues to grow, particularly as a result of Catholic immigrants arriving from Mexico Catholics are experiencing a crisis in leadership. In 2003, 3,040 parishes out of 19,081 in the United States did not have resident priests.[6] The number of Catholic nuns decreased from 90,809 in 1995 to 73,316 in 2003.[7] Caregivers who wish to interact with the faith leader of many Catholic churches, therefore, may only be able to work with a Deacon rather than a priest.

While Christianity includes official denominations, it also embraces numerous breakaway sects, orthodox movements within denominations and sects, unorthodox movements, and extra-church groups that consider themselves Christian. By far, the fastest growing subgroup of Christians are *non-denominational*, those that have not formally aligned themselves within an official denomination. Non-denominational churches establish their own policies and styles of worship without guidance from regional, national, or multinational organizations. Members of non-denominational churches often consider themselves simply "Christians." Some settle into a congregation, and others go from church to church with compatible beliefs.

Beliefs vary widely among Protestant Christian groups. Some place great emphasis on the sinfulness of humanity. Others more strongly emphasize the love of God as redemptive. Several denominations are currently experiencing widening diversity in beliefs between "conservatives," "moderates," and "liberals." Conservatives tend to see the faith as exclusivist, with an explicit confession of faith in Jesus Christ as Savior and Lord as the only path to God. Liberals recognize that reconciliation in the world takes place in a unique way through Jesus Christ but leave more room for God's grace in terms of salvation.

Different historical movements within Christianity have led to distinctions in current Christian practice. The following descriptions are very basic, but they may be useful as aids to understanding various denominations. The life of Jesus, as it is described in the New Testament, reflects all the following aspects, but Christian denominations tend to focus more on one aspect than the others.

Contemplative Christians focus on prayer, silent meditation, and personal intimacy with God. The Catholic Church and Quakers have provided numerous opportunities for practicing this type of Christianity. Denominations that identify with *The Holiness Movement* focus on removal of sinful habits and restoration of virtuous lives. The early Methodist Church and the Nazarene Church represent this branch of Christianity. *Charismatics* focus on the active presence of the Holy Spirit and gifts of the Spirit. The Assembly of God Church and its branches exemplify this kind of Christianity. *The Social Justice Movement* focuses on social change such as reducing racism, poverty, and disease in response to Jesus' mandate to love God and one another. The more mainline denominations such as the United Methodist Church, Disciples of Christ, Presbyterian Church, and some branches of the Episcopal Church emphasize social justice. *Evangelicals* focus on bible study, personal witness, and evangelism, and represent the greatest contemporary area of growth among Christians. The Southern Baptist Church and Independent Bible Churches are representative of this type of Christianity.[8]

Quakers differ from the above groups in that they focus on "Meetings" for worship and enlightenment. Quakers have no theological dogma, sacred books, creeds, designated clergy, worship images, or rituals such as baptism. They do not believe in an after-life. Quakers are committed to non-violence in thought, word and deed. Those who practice this faith are called *Friends*. Friends are open to learn from practitioners of other faiths. Both locally and internationally, Friends work with other religious and secular organizations to promote peace and justice, health care, strong ethics, public service, and responsible use of world resources.

The *Mennonite* and *Amish* faith communities developed out of the Anabaptist movement in Europe, which challenged the Protestant Reformation lead by Martin Luther as not restrictive enough. They primarily focused on adult baptism (believer's baptism) rather than infant baptism. They settled in Pennsylvania, with the highest concentration of them still in Pennsylvania and Ohio. The Amish eventually broke off from the Mennonites because they believed that the Mennonites were not restrictive enough. Both groups are known for their advocacy for peace. They do not participate in the military, and some do not pay the percentage of income tax that would support military purposes.

With their emphasis on simplicity in life style, Old Order Amish reject any change or innovation that they believe makes life more complex. They drive horses and buggies rather than cars. They do not have electricity or phones in their homes because these could connect them to the world through complex electronic and communications systems. Most are educated in the home or in one-room schools, and many receive no formal education beyond the eighth grade. They dress plainly and do not participate in photography, believing it to be a form of "graven image" forbidden by the second of the Ten Commandments. They reject Social Security and other governmental benefits.

The Church of Jesus Christ of Latter Day Saints, commonly called the *Mormon Church,* considers itself Christian, but many Christians do not consider it such because of its reliance on the *Book of Mormon: Another Testament of Jesus Christ* as the fifth Gospel. Mormons consider God and Jesus as two distinct but glorified entities (rather than two aspects of the same entity in orthodox Christianity), and believe the writings of Joseph Smith and other latter day prophets have added to the truths proclaimed by Jesus.[9]

Caregivers must not assume that one congregation of a particular denomination or Christian group is like another. It may be of little value to ask Christians which branch of Christianity they practice. It is more important to willingly hear how a particular client's or patient's faith has been a help or a hindrance in the healing process.

Basic Beliefs and Rituals

Supreme Being

- The roots of Christianity are in Judaism, and, like Jews, Christians believe that One God is the Creator of all.

- Christians acknowledge that the Spirit of God was at work through the Jewish patriarchs, prophets, and priests, but that through sending Jesus, God revealed that God is accessible to all humankind.

- Christians believe that God is primarily known through the historical life of Jesus of Nazareth, who was both human and divine, a representative of both God and humanity. This dual nature is represented by the terms Christ, the Messiah ("anointed" in Greek), or the Lord. In the term *Jesus Christ,* "Jesus" refers to the man and "Christ" refers to the Spirit of God within Jesus.

Images and Symbols

- The *cross*, the most universally accepted symbol of Christians, symbolizes the killing of Jesus (nailed to a cross until he became asphyxiated and died), after which God raised him from the dead.

- The Catholic *crucifix* places Jesus on the cross as he dies to atone or pay for the sins of humankind. Protestants generally used empty crosses to represent Jesus' resurrection.

- The *fish,* as an ancient Christian symbol, was used to identify Christians to each other during the years after Jesus' death when Christians were being persecuted. The first letters of the Greek words for *Jesus Christ, God's Son,* and *Savior* spell the Greek word for *fish*. It also may have been chosen as a symbol because Jesus told His followers that they were to be "fishers of men." It is still used today.

- Common symbols of the Holy Spirit include wind, fire, and the dove.

- Catholics pray the *Stations of the Cross,* charting the moments of Jesus' pilgrimage as he carried the cross from condemnation to death. These prayers help Catholics reflect on the meaning of Jesus' death.

- The *Rosary* is a meditative prayer, repeated by Catholics, that focuses on the life of Jesus through Mary, his mother. The prayer repeats the Our Father and Hail Mary prayers, and generally is prayed while holding a circlet of beads.

Scriptures/Sacred Texts

- The *Old Testament* of the *Bible* includes what Jews call the Torah, the Former and Latter Prophets, and the Writings. Christian Old Testaments commonly identify the same books as the Law, the Historical Books, the Prophets, and the Writings.

- The *New Testament* of the *Bible* presents Jesus as the Messiah, the most complete revelation of God, and the initiation of the Christian Church.

  - The four *Gospel*s, Matthew, Mark, Luke, and John, are accounts of Jesus' life and ministry that interpret his teachings during the first century after his death.

  - The *Acts* describe the formation of the early church.

  - The *Letters* address formation and issues of early churches.

  - The *Revelation* describes Jesus' return to earth in triumph over evil. Some groups believe this prediction of Jesus' return is literal; others believe it is symbolic of peace eventually reigning over violence.

- For Christians, the Word of God is Jesus Christ himself, but it also is common to describe the Bible as the written Word of God. The contents of the Bible include writings of more than 40 people believed to have been inspired by God through the guidance of the Holy Spirit.

- Mormons use additional scriptures including *The Book of Mormon: Another Testament of Jesus Christ, The Pearl of Great Price*, and *The Doctrine and Covenants,* based on the revelations of Joseph Smith, believed by Mormons to be a "latter-day prophet." Mormons believe the church originally established by Jesus disintegrated. Eventually, it was restored through the revelations of prophets like Joseph Smith and others who are believed to have held the same authority originally bestowed on Jesus and the original twelve disciples.[10]

- The Amish rely on both the Bible and their local district's (congregation's) *Ordnung,* an oral tradition of values that regulate how they are to conduct their lives. The males in the district determine the content of its Ordnung. While the Amish consider the roles of males and females equal but different, the males have final decision-making authority.

Basic or Core Beliefs

- Christians believe that God created human beings without sin, but sin soon entered a perfect world through human disobedience. They believe God sent Jesus to reconcile God and humanity, and to model the compassion of God.

- Evangelical Christians expect converts to be "born again" or "saved," an experience that includes professing that Jesus Christ is the Son of God who came for their salvation and promising to seek to live like Jesus. Christians believe that God demonstrated redemptive love for human beings by sending Jesus to live, teach, die, and be resurrected, and they aspire to demonstrate that same love toward others.

- Catholics believe the Spirit of Christ has been passed down through the Catholic (Universal) Church, first through St. Peter, through the early church fathers, and currently through the Popes. Protestants do not emphasize the authority of the church structure as much as they do the believer's relationship with God through the Holy Spirit, most often experienced through prayer.

- The *Trinity* refers to Father, Son, and the Holy Spirit as three manifestations of the One God. God and the Holy Spirit were present before Jesus and after Jesus.

Common Christian Rituals:

- *Baptism* symbolizes the washing away of sin and being "born again" into a new life with sins forgiven. Some Christian congregations sprinkle a few drops of water on the baptism candidate's head; others dip the candidate in water or fully immerse the candidate. Catholics and some Protestants baptize infants (*christening*) by sprinkling water on the child's head. Groups that practice infant baptism believe that original sin is present at birth. Other denominations believe that baptism is not required until a child is old enough to comprehend the significance of the ritual.

- *Confirmation* is a ritual used by groups that baptize infants to represent the beginning of the adult Christian life when young persons are old enough to understand the meaning of Christ's life, death, and resurrection.

- *Eucharist* or *communion* is the sacred act of partaking of a small amount of bread and wine or grape juice to remember the sacrifice of Jesus' body and blood for the salvation of sinners. Catholics believe that Christ becomes present in the elements during the Eucharist. Protestants consider it symbolic. Visitors are encouraged to ask if they are allowed to participate in the Eucharist or communion. Non-Catholics cannot participate in the *Eucharist* in Catholic churches. Protestant denominations vary. Most protestant churches discourage children from taking communion until they have been baptized.

- *Confession and reconciliation* are the acts of expressing remorse for sins against God and other persons, and seeking forgiveness. These are considered crucial components of Christian life.

- *Prayer* generally refers to direct communication or meditation with God or Jesus. Catholics do not worship Mary or the Saints, but many believe God to be more likely to hear the prayers of Mary or the saints, so they ask them to intercede to God on their behalf.

Spiritual Leaders

- *Pastors, ministers, and preachers* are the spiritual leaders of most Protestant Christian Churches. Some denominations have a hierarchy of leadership. For example, United Methodists also have *district superintendents* and *bishops.*

- *The Pope, cardinals, archbishops, bishops, and parish priests* are the spiritual leaders of Catholic Christians.

- *Priests* also are the spiritual leaders of Eastern Orthodox Christians and Episcopalians.

- Mormon clergy are called *bishops, first counselors, and second counselors.*

Sites of Worship

- *Churches* and *parishes* are congregations of Christian believers, although the building itself is also referred to as a church.

- Larger Catholic churches are called *cathedrals.* A group of congregations and other Catholic organizations in a particular geographical area and under the care of a *bishop* or *archbishop* is referred to as a *diocese* or *archdiocese.*

- Mormons worship in *churches* and *parishes* within a geographical *ward*, several of which make up a *stake.* Some Mormon rituals, such as baptism for the dead, eternal marriage, and sealing together parents and children are performed only in *Mormon temples.*

- Quaker meetings, usually on Sunday mornings, may be held anywhere.

- Mennonite and Amish worship is often conducted in homes. Each congregation is referred to as a *district* and is autonomous from other districts.

Worship Day(s) of the Week

- *Sunday* is the most common day of worship, representing the day of the week that Jesus Christ was resurrected after being crucified on Friday. However, weekday services are offered in many churches. Wednesday evening services are common in many Protestant churches.

- *Catholic masses* are offered several times on Sunday and throughout the week.

- *Seventh Day Adventists* worship on Saturday because beginning with Sunday, the seventh day is Saturday.

Special Days/Dates/Anniversaries

- *Easter* is the holiest day for Christians, representing the day of Christ's resurrection. The date of Easter varies each year because it is the first Sunday after the first full moon after the spring equinox. Easter is often near the Jewish Passover.

- *Lent,* a season commencing on *Ash Wednesday,* 40 days before Easter, is a period of reflection for Christians. During this time, they are asked to remove things in their lives that prevent them from experiencing the fullness of Christian life, or to add things that will help them experience greater fullness. The Thursday evening before Easter is *Maundy Thursday*, commonly believed to represent Jesus' last supper to celebrate the Jewish Passover. The day of his death is *Good Friday*.

- *Advent* is the season beginning with the fourth Sunday before Christmas and ending with Christmas, December 25. It commemorates Jesus' birth.

- *Pentecost* is observed 50 days after Passover and represents the coming of the Holy Spirit. At the original Pentecost, 50 days after Jesus' resurrection, Christians who previously spoke different languages were able to understand each other. This symbolizes that the love and compassion of God reaches all peoples.

Prohibitions

- Protestant Christians have few specified prohibitions, but generally are encouraged to model their lives after Jesus and to abide by the teachings of the New Testament.

- Catholics traditionally have prohibited behaviors that interrupt life, including suicide, euthanasia, abortion, the death penalty, and birth control (although in practice, many Catholics support birth control). Many Protestant Churches also share these prohibitions, with the exception of birth control. Some denominations and groups are more willing than others to consider these issues on a case by case basis.

- A small minority of Christian groups, primarily Pentecostal and other fundamentalist groups, have strict prohibitions including:
  - Women and youth may not serve in positions of leadership;
  - Women and girls are not to cut their hair, wear make-up, or wear provocative clothing, including trousers;
  - Dancing;
  - Playing cards;
  - Attending movies.

- Jehovah's Witnesses and Christian Science believers (Church of Christ, Scientist) are forbidden to give or receive blood transfusions.

- Jehovah's Witnesses do not observe baptism or communion, nor do they participate in most traditional and cultural celebrations such as birthdays, Christmas, Independence Day, etc.

- All Christian groups oppose abuse of alcohol and other drugs. Some prohibit all use of alcohol, while others are tolerant of alcohol use as long as it is used legally and with moderation. Seventh Day Adventists and Mormons are particularly health-conscious and abstain from nicotine, caffeine, and alcohol. Adventists abstain from eating pork and shellfish, and many are vegetarians.

- The Amish, Mennonites, and many Quakers and Seventh Day Adventists are conscientious objectors to war. The Amish, however, would not identify themselves as "pacifists" because this would involve them in a political movement.

- The Amish do not "participate in the world." They seek lives of simplicity excluding use of electricity, automobiles, etc.

Death and Dying Issues

Christian families generally want to be with their loved one at the time of death to say goodbye and to be present as the soul departs the body.

Catholics believe that baptism (most common during infancy), final confession, and absolution (forgiveness for those who confess and repent their sins) are important before death. Every effort is made to assure that the dying person has the opportunity to participate in confession and absolution with a priest before death occurs. These acts are done in private. If a Catholic chaplain or priest is not available to baptize someone about to die, any person may do so by pouring water on the head and stating, "I baptize you in the name of the Father, and of the Son, and of the Holy Spirit." A priest should always be notified after this ritual has been performed by someone other than a priest.

Death Notification

Practicing Christians will be most comfortable if their own pastor or priest makes the notification. They may or may not desire the presence of a police or hospital chaplain who is not known to them. No immediate rituals are required for Protestants. Catholics may seek absolution for the deceased from a priest as soon as possible after the death, if last rites were not given prior to death.

Anatomical Donation and Autopsy

Christians have no faith-based prohibitions against donating organs for the use of others with the exception of Jehovah's Witnesses and Christian Scientists, who forbid organ donation and any exchange of blood with another person. Nor is there a prohibition against autopsy in Christianity, although when required by law, the family should always be told why the autopsy is necessary and how it will be conducted. Neither anatomical donation nor autopsy is believed to prohibit or hinder the passage of the soul or spirit from the body.

Body Preparation

- Cremation is acceptable in most Protestant traditions as a demonstration of stewardship of earth space and financial resources. It is neither encouraged nor discouraged. Catholics and African-Americans of Caribbean descent may be more reticent to cremate.
- Christians are more likely than other faiths included in this document to want the body prepared so that it looks as if the departed is sleeping. This may emphasize the belief that for the spirit of a Christian, there is no death.
- The body usually is transported to a funeral home where body fluids are replaced with preservatives, a procedure called *embalming.*
- If the body is to be viewed before or during the funeral, make-up is applied to the face, arms, and hands. Hair is washed and styled, and ordinary clothing is placed on the body. While most funeral directors are willing to allow family members or their designees to participate in preparation of the body, most Christians decline. Christians who are African immigrants may be more likely to participate.
- Once prepared, bodies are sometimes on display for viewing at the funeral home a few days before the funeral. A *wake* or *visitation*

offers family and friends time to view the body and offer condolences to the bereaved family. Those who wish to may touch the body, as it is considered clean. Many Christian families place photos and other mementos of the deceased around or near the casket. Latin American wakes often last two days at a minimum.

Funeral Practices

- Many Christians choose to have the funeral of their loved one in their own church, while others choose a funeral home. If the body is present, it is called a *funeral*. If the body is buried or cremated before the service, it is called a *memorial service.*

- Traditionally, Christian mourners have worn black to funerals and memorial services, but this has become more relaxed in recent years with some families specifically requesting that bright colors be worn.

- The casket may be opened before the funeral, after the funeral, or both to allow family and friends to say goodbye. Other families prefer that the casket remain closed.

- A wide variety of funeral practices are acceptable, and funeral directors usually are willing to do what the family chooses. Styles of music vary. African migrants may want wakes that last one or two days and funerals that include ritualistic drumming, singing, and dancing. Some services include a sermon by the pastor or priest, while others include only remembrances of the loved one spoken by anyone who wishes to speak. Most Catholic funerals are incorporated into a Mass of Christian Burial, but some are more informal.

- Christian Scientists (Church of Christ, Scientist) tend to ignore death, although they recognize bereavement. They generally do not hold funerals.

- Amish funerals are usually conducted in the home without eulogy, flowers, or display of the body. The casket is plain, without adornment, and a simple tombstone is erected after burial. Amish women are often buried in their wedding dresses (which had been handmade, usually in blue or purple, and closed with straight pins rather than buttons or zippers.)

Burial Practices

- If not cremated, Christians are usually buried in the ground at a public cemetery following a brief committal service that typically includes a scripture, prayer, and brief comments by clergy. The casket is lowered into a vault to protect the casket and body from water and air.

- Some are placed in a mausoleum, an above ground structure with drawers for the caskets.

- Historically, local churches had their own cemeteries for members, but most municipalities and states have outlawed this practice.

Beliefs About the Afterlife

- Protestant Christians believe the spirit or soul of their loved one is either immediately transposed into Heaven at the moment of death or sleeps until the second coming of Christ.

- Christians do not speculate a great deal about what Heaven is like because, while they believe that God and Jesus are there, they consider description beyond the realm of human understanding. Some believe in a bodily resurrection with Christians receiving a new, perfect body. Others believe that only the spirit goes to Heaven.

- Catholics believe that those who die before confessing their sins reside in purgatory until they are relieved of all imperfections before entering Heaven. The intercessory prayers of the living can decrease the deceased's time in purgatory. This concept is based on writings in the Book of Maccabees, which was written 100 years or more before Jesus' birth.[11]

- While many Christians believe in Hell as an afterlife separated from God, denominations vary widely on whether or not it is a place of eternal fire and the presence of Satan or the Devil. Mormons believe that *all* souls return to Heaven to be judged by God where they are resurrected to varying degrees of glory, the highest being the celestial kingdom where the deceased lives with God, Jesus, and their families.[12]

- Christians do not believe in reincarnation.

Justice Issues

Most Christians do not understand vehicular fatalities, homicides, and other crimes to be a part of "God's plan" or ordained by God as punishment for the victim. Instead, these tragedies are seen as natural consequences of sin or evil, manifested in bad choices on the part of offenders. Some Christians, however, believe that God ordains negative consequences in certain circumstances.

Beliefs About Justice

While most Christians believe that God can, and sometimes does intervene, the degree to which God intervenes in human life is far from clear. Christians generally see no conflict between God being responsible for final justice and their participation in the criminal or civil justice systems. In emphasizing their support of legal justice, many point to the Scripture, "And what does the Lord require of you but to do justice, to love kindness, and to walk humbly with God?"(Micah 6:8).

Beliefs About Revenge

- While some Christians adhere to the Old Testament concept of "An eye for an eye and a tooth for a tooth," more significance is placed on God's grace toward sinners who recognize their sin and repent.
- Christians believe justice, not revenge, is important. Many Christians would like for their offenders to confess their sin, repent, and seek God's forgiveness. At the same time, they understand that offenders are responsible to the justice system and to victims and their families.

Beliefs About Forgiveness

- Believing Jesus paid for their sins and forgave them when they were undeserving (*grace*), many Christians believe they are obligated to forgive those who have offended them. They may attempt to let go of their anger, trusting that God will deal justly with the offender.
- Others are offended at the thought of forgiving their offender unless the offender recognizes his or her sin, is remorseful, and changes.
- Forgiveness is a very complex issue for Christians. While it may be

offered freely for minor infractions, it is more difficult for serious offenses such as homicides.

Reporting Crime

Most Christians will not hesitate to report crime unless they are minorities or immigrants who have felt oppressed by law enforcement, either in their country of origin or in this country. They may not report to law enforcement due to fear of not being believed or being deported. This is more a cultural issue than a spiritual issue.

Evidence Collection

Christians have no faith-based prohibitions against evidence collection.

Family Reactions to Crime

Spiritual reactions vary among Christian families and are commonly related to their understandings of forgiveness.

Testifying in Court

Christians who focus on forgiveness may be less likely to testify effectively than those who focus on justice. Nearly all will be willing to testify, but the effectiveness of their testimony may be influenced by their faith position.

The Amish faith forbids the swearing of oaths in court. They may make "affirmations of truth."

Presenting Victim Impact Statements

The same principles noted about testimony apply to impact statements. Caregivers may want to encourage Christians to speak honestly about the pain a murder or homicide has caused them rather than opinions about the outcome for offenders.

Restitution

Christians will have few reservations about seeking restitution for actual expenses related to the crime. Some are more hesitant to seek civil remedies because no amount of money can compensate for their suffering.

Summary

- Christians believe that Jesus Christ, born 2,000 years ago to Mary, was a manifestation of the One God in human form. His purpose was to teach humanity about God's love for all and to provide for salvation through belief in him as the Son of God.
- Spiritual practices among the 2,000 branches of Christianity vary widely.
- Jehovah's Witnesses and Christian Scientists are forbidden to give or receive blood transfusions.
- Seventh Day Adventists and Mormons abstain from nicotine, caffeine, and alcohol.
- Seventh Day Adventists abstain from pork and shellfish; many are vegetarians.
- Cremation is acceptable to most Protestants but not to most Catholics.
- Christians generally have few qualms about engaging in common justice practices in the United States, although the issue of forgiveness can be complex for many.

Things I Want To Remember From This Chapter

7
Islam

This brief description of Islam is not intended to be exhaustive. The authors recognize that within each faith there are divergent viewpoints. While we respect each individual's beliefs, it is impossible to represent all viewpoints in this limited forum. Therefore, the following information should serve only as a starting point for engaging Muslim clients or patients.

Islam is an Arabic word that means "submission to the will of God." Islam is a way of life based on inquiry, reflection, and total submission to the will and purpose of One God, called *Allah* in Arabic. Allah is another name for the same God of Judaism and Christianity. Many Arabic-speaking Jews and Christians also use the word *Allah* when referring to God. In this document, the term *God/Allah* is used to accommodate both terms.

Those who practice Islam are called *Muslims.* The word *Muslim* means "one who has submitted his or her will to God/Allah's will."

There are more than a billion Muslims in the world, and most of them do not live in the Middle East. One of every four people on earth currently practices Islam. Islam is one of the fastest growing faiths in the United States, currently numbering six to ten million, based on varying estimates.[1] Approximately 30 to 40 percent of Muslims in the United States are African American.[2] By 2010, the American Muslim population is expected to be the second largest faith practiced in the United States, second only to Christianity, according to the U.S. Department of State.

During Prophet Muhammad's lifetime in the late 5th century, Muslims became both a religious and political community, with the Prophet as the head of state. Therefore, in Islam, there is no distinction between the religious or political spheres of life. It is not so much a belief system as a way of life. Muslims understand that all of life is unified, interconnected, and ultimately divinely balanced, a concept called *Tawheed* (oneness of God).

Muslims believe that Islam actually began with the creation of the world when God/Allah sent messengers to explain how to serve Him and thereby achieve peace. These messengers included, among others: Adam, Noah, Abraham, Ishmael, Isaac, Jacob, Solomon, Moses, Jesus, and Muhammad. Muslims, like Jews and Christians, consider themselves genealogical and spiritual descendants of Abraham. The two lineages connect through the two sons of Abraham: Ishmael and Isaac. The line of Ishmael leads to Muhammad. The line of Isaac leads to Jesus. Muhammad, born in western Arabia in 571 C.E., is believed by Muslims to be the final messenger and prophet for all time.

Muslims follow many different schools of application, but they all share The Five Pillars of Islam and the Six Articles of Faith. The two largest branches of Islam are the *Sunni* and the *Shi'a* (Shiite). Shi'a Muslims accept the revelations of Muhammad but also highly revere the concepts of Muhammad's son-in-law, Ali, who was positioned by Shi'a as the first Caliph in Islam. About 90% of Muslims worldwide are Sunnis and the remaining 10% are Shi'a, the overwhelming majority of them residing in Iran and to a lesser extent in Iraq and neighboring countries. *Sufism,* the mystical expression of Islam, is found among both Sunnis and Shiites, although more commonly among Sunnis. Sunnis emphasize direct relationship between the believer and Allah, while Shiites utilize a hierarchical authority structure of legal scholars who interpret the Qur'an for the believers.

Basic Beliefs and Rituals

Supreme Being

- God/Allah is the Ultimate Truth to whom nothing can be compared.
- God/Allah does not physically give seed to bear a child, nor is God/Allah the child of anyone. (This is in contrast with Jesus in Christianity.)
- All worldly authority, leadership, and wealth belong to and are subject to God/Allah.
- God/Allah is the ultimate judge over every human behavior and

the ultimate finality. Muslims believe that human beings hold only temporal authority.

- God/Allah is described with 99 names that refer to various attributes, although the list is not considered exhaustive. Some of these descriptions include The One, All Powerful, Creator, Sustainer, Most Gracious, and Most Merciful, The Supreme Sovereign, The Protector and Guardian, The Compeller, The Abaser, The One who Raises to Honor, The One who Humiliates, The Provider of Sustenance, The Perfectly Strong, The Responder, The Absolute Reckoner, The One who Grants Life, The Death Giver, The One who has Charge Over All, and The Last.

- Muslims may repeat the 99 names for God with a rosary-type string of 100 beads called a *misbah*. The one larger bead symbolizes God.

Images and Symbols

- No single symbol universally signifies Islam. A star with a crescent to its left is often used.

- The Prophet Muhammad's flag includes the Declaration of Faith, another common symbol of Islam. It is white Arabic calligraphy on a black background. The declaration reads, "I declare there is nothing worthy of worship except for Allah, the one God, and that Mohammad is his messenger and servant."

- *Makkah* (Mecca) is the holiest city of Islam, and the *Ka'aba*, a building in Mecca made of cinderblocks draped in black silk, is held in very high regard by Muslims. The Ka'aba is built on the location where Abraham built his first temple to worship the One God.

- Other key sites include the Prophet's mosque at Medina and the Qur'an.

- Printed literature may include a simple picture or sketch of a mosque, but no images of Allah or faith leaders are allowed. This is especially true of an image of the Prophet Muhammad or any of the other prophets. Most Muslims would be offended if given an alleged picture of Muhammad because it could lead to worship of a human being. Muhammad is not to be worshipped.

- While human representations are generally prohibited, such as photos in brochures, (except for medical texts and children's literature), an entire body of Islamic art including mosaics, geometrical and symmetrical designs, and Arabic calligraphy and illumination is practiced and honored in Muslim culture.

Scriptures/Sacred Texts

- The *Qur'an*, considered literally divine and inerrant, is the definitive sacred text of Muslims. God began revealing the Qur'an through the Angel Gabriel to Prophet Muhammad, the "Messenger of God," in *Makkah* (Mecca) when he was about 40. The revelation began in 610 C.E. and continued until Muhammad's death in 632 C.E. after he had established the first Muslim state in Medina. Both Mecca and Medina are in the Western Arabian Peninsula. Muhammad was believed to be illiterate during the time of these revelations.

  - Muslims believe that the only true Qur'an is in Arabic, but several English translations have been made.

  - The Qur'an is divided into 114 chapters called *Surahs,* and each Surah has verses.

  - Muslims refer to themselves, Christians, and Jews as "People of the Book," believing that each Holy Book revealed by God/Allah was a chapter in the same book.

  - Though revered by Muslims as the last of God's prophets, Muhammad is not worshipped but is understood only as a human messenger.

- The second source from which Muslims derive their religious teachings is the *Hadith*, a validated collection of the sayings, practices, and allowances or prohibitions of the Prophet Muhammad.

- Other sources of Islamic law include *Ijma* (the consensus of scholars), *Qiyas* (analogical deductions of scholars), and *Ijtihad* (personal, deductive, creative thinking when no precedent exists in other sources.) Only those who have studied Islamic law are familiar with the details of these sources.

Basic or Core Beliefs

- One becomes a Muslim by declaring and believing that "There is no God but God, and Muhammad is the Messenger of God."

- The ultimate concern of every Muslim is to be offered a place in Heaven rather than Hell. Muslims believe that Heaven can be hoped for through good actions and intentions. However, God/ Allah's mercy also may be given based on no particular actions or intentions.

- The basic practices of Islam include the Five Pillars of Islam, or *arkaan*. These include:

  - Stating and living the principle that there is no object of devotion except God, and Muhammad is the Messenger of God (*tawheed* or *shahadah*).

  - Engaging in ritual prayer five times each day (*salat*) while facing Mecca, the holy city of Islam. Symbolic physical cleansing precedes each prayer. (In addition, Muslims can offer personal prayers any time.)

  - Cleansing one's yearly wealth by separating out 2 ½ percent of accumulated net assets and savings, and giving it to the poor (*zakat*). Since Muslims are already obligated to care for their close relatives, Zakat is giving outside their closest family. Many mosques (*masajid*) in the United States have a Zakat Fund that can be utilized to help those in need. Though it is not a form of Zakat, many Muslims living in the United States send large amounts of their income to support more distant relatives in countries lacking social security or welfare.

  - Fasting (for those beyond puberty) from dawn to sunset during Ramadan, the ninth month of the lunar calendar (*sawm*).

  - Making a pilgrimage to Mecca once in one's lifetime if physically and financially able (*hajj*). The pilgrimage centers on the *Ka'aba,* the cube-shaped "House of God" believed to have been built by Abraham and his son, Ishmael.

- The Six Articles of Belief include:
  - Belief in God/Allah.
  - Belief in the angels.
  - Belief that God/Allah revealed Holy Books to Prophets including the *Mushaf* to Abraham, the *Psalms* to David, the *Torah* to Moses, the *Gospel* to Jesus, and the *Qur'an* to Muhammad.
  - Belief in all the Prophets of God throughout the ages, ending with Muhammad.
  - Belief in a judgment day when no deed, great or small, will be overlooked and will be judged by God/Allah.
  - Belief that *Qadr* and *Qada'*, the major turning points in one's life, are ordained before birth. Less significant events are based on free will or choice, but God/Allah knows what those choices will be.
- *Jihad* (to struggle) is a term commonly used in current discussions of Islam. It is sometimes mistakenly translated "holy struggle." Jihad includes two types: "the greater jihad" which is warfare within oneself against evil or temptation (addressed in the early Meccan chapters of the Qur'an when the total psychological transformation of the individual was God/Allah's focus), and "the lesser jihad" which is the defense of Islam or a Muslim country against aggression (addressed in the later Medinan chapters of the Qur'an when Medina existed as the first Islamic state with Muhammad as commander of the army).

Spiritual Leaders

Islam recognizes many types of spiritual leaders, but none are set aside as mediators between God/Allah and followers. Anyone of good character and knowledge can be elected to lead prayer. Higher knowledge of religion, law, methodology, and history is usually recognized, and followers begin to attach themselves to these teachers. Spiritual teachers, who may or may not be formally trained, include:

- *Amir,* principle authority in any undertaking (office may be temporary)

- *Alim*, male scholar or expert
- *Alima*, female scholar or expert
- *Faqih* or *Faqhiy,* male expert in religious law
- *Faqiha* or *Faqhiyya,* female expert in religious law
- *Qadi*, male or female judge in an Islamic court of law.
- *Imam*, leader of prayer (can include any of the above).
- *Shaikh*, spiritual leader (the same term is sometimes applied to an elder or financial leader and can include any of the above).

Sites of Worship

- Muslims pray in a mosque or *masjid*, which means "a place of bowing down." Mosques generally are simply structures with domes on top. There are no chairs in the prayer room because prayers involve several movements. In a masjid, Muslims face toward Mecca and pray. Masajid (plural of masjid) have markings on the floor to indicate the direction of prayer lines to assure that those praying are directly facing Mecca. The imam leads the prayers and addresses the congregation from a platform called the *minbar.* The top step is reserved for Muhammad and is never used by the imam. Men and women are separated during prayer by space, a short curtain, or a room divider. Several movements are included in Muslim prayers including bowing and full prostration on knees with the forehead on the ground. This posture demonstrates submission and humility before God/Allah. Some masajid are small and others are large enough to be considered complexes or Islamic Centers and may include a school, bookstore, community center, and large dining room or meeting hall. A masjid may also be called a *jami.*
- Muslim women cover their heads when entering the prayer area of a masjid, and all Muslims remove their shoes. The purpose of this is hygiene since participants will be placing their foreheads on the floor as part of the prayer ritual. Near the entrance of a masjid is a fountain or basin for ritual washing (*wudu*) before prayer.
- A room or dedicated space where people pray is called a *musala*. Muslims typically have a *musala* in their homes.

- Any clean spot can be used for prayer and, if need be, Muslims can pray in a hospital bed, on an airplane, in a car, or in a train. Value is placed more on keeping the humble appointment with God five times per day than on the place where prayer takes place.

- Both genders are expected to dress modestly at all times, but especially when entering a masjid. Muslim women cover their heads when entering the prayer area.

- Many masajid in the United States conduct public tours for non-Muslims. Most do not require visitors to cover themselves. Anyone expecting to develop a relationship with Muslim communities, however, should dress modestly with loose clothing that covers the arms and legs in order to be viewed as respectful of Muslims. Shoes should be removed when entering, but most masajid do not require visiting women to cover their heads. Visitors are not expected to participate in the ritual washing, and should not engage in prayer unless specifically invited to do so. Visitors usually sit to the back or the side during prayer.

Worship Day(s) of the Week

- Attendance at *Friday Prayer* is required of Muslim men. However, women may be excused for childcare purposes. This weekly holy time, just after the meridian of the sun on Fridays, is called *Jumuuah*. The remainder of the day may be spent in any way. To assure Muslim participation, meetings and events organized by non-Muslims should not be scheduled to interfere with Friday Jumuuah prayer time.

- In the United States, most Muslims who want to attend Friday *Jumuuah* prayer ask permission to leave their jobs during the day and make up the hours when they return. If they are not allowed to leave work, Muslims may make up the Friday prayer time at home, but this is considered an undesirable alternative and many are resistant to accepting the alternative.

- Students, workers, and professionals increasingly are requesting time to pray. Some places have responded by providing prayer space at schools, in the workplace, or other areas where large numbers of Muslims are present.

- The Prophet Muhammad fasted every Monday and Thursday. Muslims are encouraged to do the same.

- All healthy adult Muslims are required to fast one month each year during *Ramadan*, the ninth month of the lunar calendar, during which God/Allah began to reveal the Qur'an to Muhammad. The fast begins at dawn and ends at sunset each day. At sunset, Muslims are allowed to eat, drink, and have conjugal relations. Special prayers called *Taraweeh* are offered in the evening during this period. Prayers last from 45 minutes to 2 hours. The entire Qur'an, which has 30 divisions called *Juz*, is read during *Ramadan*. Muslims, consequently, get very little sleep during Ramadan.

- The date of the beginning of *Ramadan* changes approximately 11 days each year because the Islamic calendar is lunar. Although it is astronomically predicted, the exact beginning of *Ramadan* is never known until the last minute and is determined by the human sighting of the crescent or new moon.

- During the last 10 days of *Ramadan*, Muslims look for the Night of Power, or *Laylat Al-Qadr*, during which they expect God to positively answer every good prayer. Some Muslims practice living totally in a *masjid* during this period, immersing themselves in prayer and contemplation.

- The two Islamic holidays per year are referred to as "The Two Eids." *Eid Al-Fitr* is a three-day holiday with mandatory participation in an early morning prayer on the first day. *Eid Al-Fitr* celebrates the end of the month-long fast of *Ramadan*. During this time, Muslims socialize and enjoy new clothes and special foods. Children are given gifts that may include small amounts of money. For this holiday, and up to a week prior, food is collected and distributed to the poor to satisfy the requirement of Zakat Al-Fitr.

- *Eid Al-Adha* is celebrated approximately 70 days after *Eid Al-Fitr*. *Eid Al-Adha* is at the end of the month of *Hajj*. This holiday commemorates Abraham's faith when ordered by God to sacrifice his son, Ishmael. *Eid Al-Adha* is celebrated much like *Eid Al-Fitr* with the addition of sacrificing lamb, goat, cow, or camel and giving two thirds of it to the poor. It is usually during these two eids that people give their yearly dues to zakat.

- A charity called *sadaqat* can be given at any time and in any amount. Many people make a sadaqat donation when something good happens to them to express thanks to God/Allah for their good fortune. The amount of the contribution is generally based on the number of people in the household multiplied by the cost of a good meal. This gift, which goes to the poor, is often given before going to the Eid Al-Fitr Prayer.

- The *Isra'* and *Mir'aj* commemorate the one-night journey of the Prophet Muhammad from Mecca to Jerusalem, then up to the Heavens, and back to Mecca. During this journey, the Prophet met other former prophets and received the exact form of Muslim prayer.

Prohibitions

- Worshipping gods other than God/Allah.

- Suicide.

- Touching between opposite genders outside the family. A non-related man should not extend a hand to a Muslim woman.

- Being alone with someone of the opposite sex or letting a person of the opposite sex into the home when the husband or wife is not present. Except in the direst emergencies, a woman should be allowed to cover her hair before a male enters the home.

- Sharing private family information with strangers.

- Bringing shame or loss of dignity to self or family.

- Spying (except in war), backbiting, tale bearing, calling offensive names.

- Humiliating or laughing at another person.

- Eating pork or any pork extracted products such as lard, shortening that includes fat, and gelatin in desserts and candies. This includes bacon bits in many salads. Food prohibitions also include any animal that has died from disease, and any food that has been blessed in the name of or dedicated to another god besides the common God worshipped by Jews, Christians, and Muslims.

Shellfish is not prohibited but is considered "makruh," meaning, "not recommended;" therefore, eating it is not considered a major sin.

- Alcohol.

- Sex before marriage.

- Adultery.

- Homosexuality.

- Refusing to consent to a divorce simply to annoy the spouse. Both men and women can initiate divorce, but divorce is discouraged.

- Moving physically in public with an intention of drawing lurid attention to one's self.

- Covering the face is not required in the Qur'an except for the wives of Muhammad. Muslim women are to wear loose fitting opaque clothing that does not reveal body shape and that covers everything except the face, hands, and feet. Older women may remove the mandated covering, but it is better for them to continue in compliance. The Qur'an does not give anyone at the family or state level permission to force a woman to cover. It is the woman's choice. Women who choose to cover are complying with the three mandates for covering in the Qur'an itself.

- Men also are commanded to wear loose fitting opaque clothing to cover their bodies from the navel to the knee. Muslims have high regard for modesty in both men and women.

- Even though Muslim men are allowed up to four wives, the Qur'an warns men against marrying more than one wife. If they do, they must treat all the wives justly, which is nearly impossible. Polygamy is now seldom practiced, particularly where it violates public law, such as in the United States. The ancient intent of polygamy was to assure that women were cared for during times when men were few, such as after a war.

- God/Allah forbids all forms of inequity, tyranny, and oppression.

- Giving false witness against someone is equal to murder.

Death and Dying Issues

Muslims believe that God/Allah directs all aspects of life and death, insuring a divinely balanced world. In the Qur'an, God/Allah refers to life on earth as "an illusion filled with competition and boasting." Enlightened people learn to recognize its minimal value. Allah creates human beings, determines their life span, and causes them to die. Death is seen as a simple passing from one stage of life, the testing stage, to the eternal stage. When a family member becomes ill, it is seen as an opportunity to receive blessings by taking care of him or her. Caring for an elderly parent is seen as a most blessed opportunity because children can never adequately repay parents for all they have done for them. Facing death with patience and fortitude, be it peaceful or violent, will be rewarded.

Death Notification

- An Imam (Leader of Prayer) of any ethnicity or a Muslim spiritual leader of the same ethnicity should deliver the notification if possible.

- Immediate notification is imperative. Muslims are to be buried in the ground within 24 hours, but no more than 48 hours, after death.

- Family members should be asked about their preference regarding religious attention. Some families may identify themselves as Muslim but live secularly and not practice Islam.

- Reference to untimely death should be avoided. The Qur'an instructs that the time, place, and manner of death are written for each person when the soul is infused into the body before birth.

Anatomical Donation

- Organ donations are generally allowed but the idea is difficult at best. Some Muslims will have written organ donation into their living wills, but most will be confused by being asked to donate organs and will seek out an imam or teacher for advice. Muslim scholars from around the world who meet every few years in Mecca have deemed donating organs acceptable. Most Muslims are unaware, however, that these scholars have now approved organ donation.

- All body parts are believed to become reunited with the soul and will stand before God/Allah on Judgment Day. Therefore, burying an incomplete body is of little consequence to Muslims, although if missing parts are later identified, the family will probably want them interred with the body.

Autopsy

- Autopsy is unacceptable unless required by law. When necessary, it should occur as soon as possible after death so as not to delay burial beyond 24-48 hours.
- Violating practices of modesty for the deceased's body, which include covering the body from chest to knees, is disturbing to Muslims. The body should be kept covered when not being examined during autopsy or any other procedure.

Body Preparation

- Muslims do not embalm.
- Cremation is forbidden.
- The soul, after briefly leaving the body, returns to the body where it remains until Judgment Day. Therefore, the soul may be present during the required body washing ritual.
- The ritual of body washing is part of an emphasis on cleanliness called *Taharah*. Washing may be performed at a hospital, morgue, funeral home, or mosque where a license has been issued. A group of Muslim washers, usually volunteers, includes an odd number of people of the same gender. An exception to the "same sex" rule is made when husbands choose to wash their wives or wives choose to wash their husbands. The body is treated with extreme care, as if fragile or breakable, and every effort is made not to injure or harm it.
  - Jewelry and clothing are removed, and a sheet is spread from chest to knee. The hands, mouth, nose, face, arms, hair,

ears, and feet of the deceased are washed with lukewarm water in the same way Muslims prepare for prayer.

- The deceased's private parts are washed in a process called *ghusl*.

- Next, the entire body is washed three times while under a sheet to respect the nakedness of the deceased. Camphor infused water is used in the final rinse. The body is then towel-dried and cotton is placed in the body's orifices. Body washers generally do not inform the family about the condition of the body. However, when the person was seriously injured or killed, it may be helpful to prepare the family for what they will see.

- The body is wrapped in unstitched white cotton cloth, or *kafan*. (The English word "coffin" is derived from *kafan*.) Several pieces of cloth may be used, depending on the size and gender of the person.

- The face is the last part of the body to be covered after washing. Before the face is covered, close family members who desire may view it. After that, no one views the body.

- After fully covering the head, strings of torn cloth are loosely tied at the head, waist, and feet to prevent the *kafan* from unraveling and to easily identify the head of the deceased.

- No objects or property are buried with the deceased.

■ Family members may participate in the ritual washing if they choose.

Funeral Practices

■ The body is placed in a closed casket and taken to the mosque or graveside.

■ The casket is positioned to face *Mecca* for the funeral, called a *janazah*. Mourners remain standing and line up in rows facing the casket to perform the *janazah* prayer, which can be prayed by a small number of people of both genders. Speeches and eulogies are not given. The deceased's lifetime practices are expected to speak for themselves.

- Wearing white at funerals is recommended, although colors may be worn according to ethnic and customary preferences.

- Screaming, excessive loud crying, tearing one's clothes, and deliberately falling on the floor are prohibited. Some Muslims feel obliged to practice these habits to satisfy cultural expectations in their countries, but these practices are discouraged in the Qur'an.

- The Qur'an instructs that all debt of the deceased be repaid, and moderation is mandated for funeral expenses. Excess money is used to pay the debt of the deceased or is given to the poor in the deceased's name.

- After the burial, relatives and community members stay with the grieving family for at least three days, the official mourning period. Beyond the three-day mourning period, relatives, friends, and community members perform daily acts for the grieving family including cooking, cleaning, and childcare for two additional weeks or more. A widow officially mourns for four months and 10 days. This period is called *iddah*. No offer of remarriage may occur until *iddah* has ended. This practice assures that if the widow is pregnant, the father of the child can be identified.

- Well-wishers often bring food to the family's home during the mourning period. All food should observe Muslim dietary restrictions. Donations to an appropriate charity in the name of the deceased also are appreciated.

- When a Muslim dies, it is appropriate to say, "From God we come and to God we return." Guests also may say, "May God forgive them and enter them into Heaven." Any prayer is acceptable for Muslim children who have reached the first trimester but not puberty. Children less than seven years old who die enter heaven with no reckoning because they are not deemed responsible for what they have done. Likewise, when a practicing Muslim dies unexpectedly by a violent death, they enter heaven unquestioned. In these cases, only the first prayer is said.

- Muslims reject physical touching from non-related, opposite gender visitors at a funeral. Restraint in this area is required at the funeral and burial as well as in all care-giving relationships. However, if family members of the deceased offer a hand, it can be shaken in return.

- Males and females often sit in different places and sometimes in unconnected rooms for the funeral. Occasionally, members of the opposite sex are sent to different buildings.

- A Qur'an reading typically is held, even if the deceased was more secular in habit. Muslim visitors are handed a small booklet containing a portion of the Qur'an to read while visiting the family of the deceased.

Burial Practices

- The body is removed from the casket at the graveside and placed on its right side with the deceased's face toward Mecca within the grave, called a *lahd*.

- Burial without a coffin is preferred because this was the practice of Prophet Muhammad. Humans are created from dirt/clay and should return to that same state. Muslims, however, comply with the law of the country where coffins and vaults are mandated. If the law mandates a coffin, the body is turned on the right side in the coffin. Effort is made to orient the gravesite so the body faces Mecca.

- Family members throw a small handful of dirt into the grave alongside the body or the coffin. Others then do likewise.

- Ostentatious graves are discouraged. Burial depth of four to six-feet in the ground is mandatory. The burial mound is kept small. A small stone may be used to mark the burial site, which may contain brief information about the deceased.

- Islamic tradition supports visiting the gravesite. Relatives visit several times each year. Some bring flowers, but most simply say prayers asking forgiveness for the deceased and for themselves.

Beliefs About the Afterlife

- Muslims believe that all human souls come from God/Allah and return to God/Allah who judges them.

- The Angel of Death, *Malaika Al Mawt,* extracts the soul from the body of the deceased (gently if the person lived a good life; violently if the person lived an evil life), and sits at the head of the deceased. The Angel addresses the soul with several questions and then takes it to the gates of Heaven where it is greeted with expectations of God's mercy (heaven) or God's wrath (hell) based on deeds performed during life. The soul then is returned to the body where it remains until Judgment Day.

- The Qur'an explains that every act of hearing, seeing, and knowing will be questioned on Judgment Day. Judgment Day will be an absolute day of justice when all actions taken by an individual will be revealed and acknowledged to the world by him or her. If the individual refuses to acknowledge sin, his or her body parts are given the ability to speak and report their actions. No one has ever known when Judgment Day will occur, not even the Prophets.

- If violent death occurred and no body is recovered, the soul and body will be reunited on Judgment Day. Every soul is promised a just and full accounting and may be entered into Heaven by God's grace alone.

- Suicide is forbidden. A person who takes his or her own life earns their rightful place in hell, continuing the suicidal act for eternity. Suicide is a mortal sin and earns eternal damnation.

- Heaven is filled with mild weather, rivers, juice that one never tires of drinking and does not cause intoxication, greenery, beautiful people with beautiful eyes, silk clothing, gold, reclining couches, and immediate gratification of every desire. Residents of Heaven will have no evil desires.

- Several acts may be performed in the name of the deceased, such as donating to schools, hospitals, and libraries, digging a water well for public consumption, or creating a continuous endowment. Acts such as these benefit the deceased until Judgment Day.

- Judgment Day is followed by eternal afterlife in one of seven heavens or seven hells. Prophets live in the Seventh Heaven. Ordinary people who practiced Islam's traditions and avoided major sin will reside in the level of heaven appropriate to their deeds.

- The prayers of children who pray for their parents to be raised to a higher level in heaven will be honored. The children, too, will be rewarded for their prayers.

Justice Issues

One of the 99 names of God/Allah is *The Just (Al-Adl)*. Islamic tradition teaches that divine justice prevails over any form of human justice. Muslims believe that evil is not inevitable and is temporary. Truth and goodness ultimately prevail. Human beings are born free of sin. As such, they have a natural, Creator-conscious inclination to good. When someone veers from the peaceful path, they can return to their natural equilibrium through repentance or with the help of others. Adam and Eve are seen as examples of humans held responsible and accountable for their actions after repenting to God. Atonement for poor choices and actions may be achieved with patience and perseverance in the face of hardship, injuries, and difficulties. Since only God knows the past, present, and future, Muslims are taught not to obsess over why things happen in a particular way in time, space, and place.

Beliefs About Justice

- Islamic ideology, philosophy, and law mandate justice and the preservation of life above all other considerations. Ultimate justice rests with God/Allah who, on Judgment Day, will mete out absolute justice. No act will be missed.

- Muslims are to be just (that is next to piety) and to fear Allah. Muslims specifically are directed to judge non-Muslims fairly when put in that position.

- The practice of truthful and just witnessing, even when a family member is involved, implies that protecting family honor is not as important as seeking and establishing justice.

- Every oppressed person deserves a hearing and has the right to seek retribution. Every person is allowed and encouraged to defend himself or herself from attack.

Beliefs About Revenge

- God/Allah is neither vengeful nor revengeful but does judge and carries out just punishment.

- Foregoing personal revenge when injustice has occurred is a sign of human greatness and leadership. The Prophet Muhammad set the example during the Reopening of Mecca *(Fatih Makkah)*. Muhammad entered his hometown in triumph, yet his relatives had previously starved him, plotted against him, and tried to kill him. He did not seek revenge against any of them, but gave them amnesty.

- Muslims are to "turn off evil with good" (13:22) but are allowed to defend themselves from oppression. Justice can be achieved through revenge, but forgiveness and imitating God's mercy are more strongly encouraged.

- God/Allah alone owns destiny and the future and is free to give, through grace, mercy to anyone, including those who seem least deserving.

- God/Allah, either in this world or the next, repays evildoers for evil.

- God/Allah holds individuals accountable, but collective punishment occurs when a large number of individuals commit evil or stay silent while evil is committed.

- Family or community members, through avoidance, non-inclusion, silence, or physical punishment, may bring a guilty person to judgment.

Beliefs About Forgiveness

- Forgiveness is praised in the Qur'an. The death penalty, therefore, may be avoided for a lesser sentence if the family of someone killed accepts compensation from the offender or prefers to forgive the offender. When a life is taken prematurely, such as during a car crash that causes the abortion of a child, Islam expects the offender to pay compensation to the mother based on the number of months between the infant's conception and death.

- God/Allah has given Himself four names relating to forgiveness. These are among the most often repeated names in the Qur'an. They provide infinite hope for repentance:
  - *Al-Tawwab*, The Ever-Forgiving or The Acceptor of Repentance
  - *Al-Afuw*, The Most Forgiving
  - *Al-Ghafoor*, The Forgiving
  - *Al-Ghafaar*, The Great Forgiver
- To be forgiven by God, a person must make *Tawbah*. This requires that the person:
  - Recognize the wrong.
  - Regret the wrong.
  - Make a sincere decision to desist from committing wrong.
  - Right the wrong.
  - Ask forgiveness of the victim(s) for the wrong.
  - Ask God/Allah's forgiveness for the wrong.
  - Reconcile with the victim of the offense if possible.
- Seeking forgiveness must be swift and sincere. A person who recommits the same sin or a similar sin again and again will not be forgiven. Asking forgiveness on one's deathbed for a life of sin does not necessarily result in forgiveness even though God/Allah may be gracious and forgive. Even when all other steps have been taken, God does not forgive the offender unless he or she has also asked the victim for forgiveness.
- A victim is not obligated to forgive the perpetrator, but doing so is commendable.
- Muslim victims do not endorse private agreements among officers of the court intended to diminish culpability for a perpetrator's actions. Plea-bargaining may be interpreted as a conspiracy within the legal system to exact injustice against the victim. On the other hand, some Muslims choose to reduce or drop charges if they believe reprisals will follow legal judgments decided in their own

favor, such as in the workplace, school, or prison.

- Muslims believe that if they accept and receive punishment on earth for a wrong, they will not face punishment for it in the hereafter.

Reporting a Crime

- Reporting a crime depends on the nature of the crime and the victim's perception of the seriousness of the crime. For example, petty theft may not be reported because the punishment would be considered more severe than the crime warrants.

- Domestic violence between spouses may not be reported but, instead, be handled within the Muslim community through family arbitration. Arbitration within the community may lead to separation of the parties. When the violence results in serious injury or death, however, Muslims recognize that the justice system will step in.

- When a Muslim does report a crime, law enforcement authorities of the same gender should respond. Officials taking crime reports, conducting interviews, or questioning Muslims should not be alone with a Muslim of the opposite sex.

- A practicing Muslim will make every attempt to truthfully detail a crime. Giving false witness against someone is forbidden and constitutes a major sin in God/Allah's system of justice.

- Muslims are called to stand up for justice regardless of the consequences. A well-known Hadith states, "If you see something wrong, try to change it with your hands; if you can't, then try to change it with your words; and if you cannot do that either, then at least have the feeling in your heart that it is wrong and this is the least of faith." Honesty is required in all business dealings.

- The Qur'an emphasizes the need to collectively work against the unjust, tyrannical, or oppressive wrongdoer until he or she returns to justice.

- Reporting crime in and by the Muslim community has decreased significantly since September 11, 2001. The attacks on America have bred suspicion and unfair treatment of the Islamic community by some ordinary citizens and the U.S. government. These actions have resulted in widespread fear of deportation or oppression toward

Middle Easterners and the Islamic community. Unfortunately, many Muslims now believe that:

- The United States government and its agencies are inherently anti-Muslim and anti-Arab. As such, it may be impossible for Muslims to receive justice.

- The government is invasive of Arab and Muslim privacy. As a result, reporting a crime by a Muslim against a Muslim, such as a case of domestic violence, may be inviting destruction of the Muslim community.

- As with all immigrants, reporting a crime within a family may result in immigration charges and deportation. Even when a Muslim victim is inclined toward seeking justice, he or she may choose not to report a crime in order to protect their citizenship or that of a family member. They fear that police and federal authorities may attempt to find minor infractions to deport everyone directly or indirectly involved in a crime. This is particularly true of recent immigrants who have left an oppressive government. Injustices suffered in their country of origin or past historical events may have engendered distrust of all authority figures.

Evidence Collection

- Male law enforcement officials should not enter the home of a Muslim woman for any reason unless an adult male family member or another woman is present. This is necessary to protect a Muslim woman's reputation. If a home must be searched, authorities should wait until a Muslim woman has had proper time to cover her head and fully dress. If the body of a suspect or party to a crime must be searched, same sex officers must perform the body search in a private place to minimize the humiliation to the person being searched.

- Muslims involved in evidence collection or a search will cooperate if they believe the authorities are trustworthy and have good intentions. If they believe the authorities are not trustworthy, they may hide information, even if it means unjustly putting themselves at risk.

- Some Muslims will respond only to what they are asked directly. They are not likely to offer additional information because they fear repercussions.

- Interviews and evidence collection should accommodate prayer times for Muslims. Muslims plan their prayers by the sun and the moon, generally in two- to three-hour portions, for example the time for "afternoon prayer" or "sunset prayer." Therefore, setting an exact time for meetings is problematic.

- Establishing a chronology of events as they occurred is a difficult concept for many people of Middle Eastern descent. Investigators and other caregivers should explain what a chronology is and how to report a detailed event in chronological order.

- Immigrant family members may have different last names. A Muslim wife does not typically take her husband's name, and a child's last name is sometimes the father's first name. Members of a family, for example, may each have a different, yet legal, name. This can be confusing for caregivers.

Family Reactions to Crime

- How families react to crime vary. Many believe that an offense committed by a family member is a private matter and should not be reported to authorities who are considered strangers.

- When difficulties arise within a marriage, the Qur'an instructs a husband and wife to appoint arbiters from each side of the family. Enlisting people from outside the extended family to investigate or solve family problems is an unfamiliar concept. Preserving family honor and avoiding family shame is seen as a major obligation.

- Recent immigrants to the United States may be especially reluctant to testify against one another and may be conflicted over what and when to report. Other members of the Islamic community believe they are obligated to speak up publicly when injustice has occurred, even when a family member has been involved.

- Failure of the legal system to fully punish wrongdoers might be understood as requiring the family to right the wrong.

Testifying in Court

- Honesty is a religious obligation. Muslims are required to testify truthfully, even against their own family members. However, some immigrants may view court proceedings with suspicion and fear because of previous experiences. They may choose not to tell the truth if they believe it will keep themselves or a family member from being deported or if they feel the system is unfair to them.

- Legal repercussions for lying under oath are not understood by some immigrants, especially those who moved away from repressive regimes where lying was a necessary method of staying alive. Legal authorities and crime victim assistance providers should explain, through a competent translator, the serious consequences of lying under oath.

- Muslims believe it is inappropriate to stare directly into the eyes of someone older or of the opposite sex. Witnesses who avoid eye contact should not be seen as dishonest or guilty.

Presenting Victim Impact Statements

- Chronological order may need to be explained to a Muslim victim of immigrant descent in order for the Victim Impact Statement to flow chronologically.

- Recent immigrants are likely to discuss the physical impact of crime but may not be as likely to describe its non-visible impact such as mental or emotional duress, which may be considered private.

- Discussing private matters publicly or with strangers is considered a weakness of character and is considered shameful. This is particularly true of recent immigrants. These ideas become increasingly less pronounced after about five years of residency, but prosecutors must understand that these views may exist without open discussion within a family, and minors may be socialized to observe the same characteristics.

Restitution

- The Qur'an instructs followers to be accountable for all actions.

Personal accountability is a major element of judgment day. Practicing Muslims are inclined to admit fault and make restitution. Muslim victims of crime seek full restitution, believing it to be a divine right.

- The facilitation of restitution and justice is required of all people in a position of authority, whether at the family, local, state, or federal level.

- The court or state is expected to make restitution if the offender is unable to do so. This expectation originates in societies where insurance is not available. Judges who do not order restitution from the state when a perpetrator is unable to pay will be seen as unjust.

- Muslims immigrants generally know nothing about crime victim compensation programs. Legal authorities and crime victim assistance providers should explain these funds and offer help to Muslims who wish to apply.

- Collective restitution is seen as incumbent upon a family in order for the family to retain public respect. This may take the form of legal redress or actions.

Summary

- Those who practice Islam are called Muslims.

- "Allah" is the Arabic name given to the same one God of Jews and Christians.

- Many complexities are involved in the combination of culture and spirituality for most of those who practice Islam.

- Among the Five Pillars of Islam are ritual prayers five times a day and fasting during Ramadan (30 days based on the lunar calendar that fall 10 days earlier each year, thus cycling through the calendar every 36 years). Caregivers must be aware of the significance of these Pillars when scheduling events.

- Muslims abstain from pork and alcohol.

- Remove shoes before entering a mosque.

- Many Muslims observe touching restrictions between the sexes, so wait to see if they offer a hand and follow their lead.

- Muslim men and women wear loosely fitting clothing that does not reveal body shape. It is respectful to wear clothing that covers much of the body and no see-through or revealing clothing when in the presence of Muslims. Many Muslim women cover their hair when in the presence of men, but they do not expect non-Muslims to do so.

- Many Muslims avoid direct eye contact between the sexes, so this should not be construed as dishonesty or avoidance.

- Muslim women generally do not take the names of their husbands, and a child's last name is often the father's first name.

- Natural crying when grieving is acceptable but loud outbursts and tearing of clothes is prohibited. (Some Muslims who practice these behaviors are doing so based on cultural rather than spiritual norms.)

- Autopsy, cremation, and embalming are strongly discouraged, but Muslims recognize the need for autopsy to seek justice.

- Suicide is forbidden in the Qur'an.

- One's place in the afterlife is determined by the degree to which the person submitted to the will of Allah. Paradise includes five levels of heaven and seven levels of hell.

- Muslims consider Islam as a way of life rather than only a religion. Therefore, there is little distinction between faith and government.

- Muslims currently feel significant mistrust of the U.S. Government, so while telling the truth is a strong mandate of Islam, they may be cautious about involvement in the justice system.

What I want to remember from this chapter

Appendix 1
Supplemental Information and Resources

General Spirituality

Barton, David. *Original Intent: The Courts, the Constitution, and Religion.* Aledo, TX: Wallbuilder Press, 2004.

Canda, Edward and Leola Furman. *Spiritual Diversity in Social Work Practice.* New York: The Free Press, 1999.

Hopfe, Lewis. *Religions of the World (6th Edition).* New York: Macmillan, 1994.

Johnson, Jay and Marsha McGee. *How Different Religions View Death and Afterlife.* Philadelphia: The Charles Press, 1998.

Koenig, Harold. *Spirituality in Patient Care.* Philadelphia: Templeton Foundation Press, 2002.

Lampman, Lisa (Ed.). *God and the Victim.* Grand Rapids, MI: William B. Eerdmans, 1999.

Magida, Arthur and Stuart Matlins. *How to be a Perfect Stranger: A Guide to Etiquette in Other People's Religious Ceremonies* (Volumes I and II). Woodstock, VT: Jewish Lights, 1996 and 1997.

Scales, T., Terry Wolfer, David Sherwood, Diana Garland, Beryl Hugen, and Sharon Pittman. *Spirituality and Religion in Social Work Practice.* Alexandria, VA: Council on Social Work Education, 2002.

Toropov, Brandon and Father Buckles Luke. *The Complete Idiot's Guide to World Religions* (2nd Edition). New York: Alpha Books, 2001.

Van Hook, Mary, Beryl Hugen, and Marian Aguilar. *Spirituality Within Religious Traditions in Social Work Practice.* Pacific Grove, CA: Brooks/ Cole, 2002.

Native American Spirituality

www.nmai.si.edu (The American Indian Museum at Smithsonian Institute)

Deloria, Jr., Vine. *God is Red: A Native View of Religion.* Golden, CO: Fulcrum Publishing, 2003.

McGaa, Ed. *Mother Earth Spirituality: Native American Paths to Healing Ourselves and the World.* New York: Harper Collins, 1990.

Neihardt, John G. *Black Elk Speaks.* Lincoln: University of Nebraska Press, 1972.

Neihardt, John G. *Indian Tales and Others.* Lincoln: University of Nebraska Press, 1926.

Turner, Frederick T. *The Portable North American Indian Reader.* New York: Viking Press, 1974.

Hinduism

www.hindu.org/ht/ *Hinduism Today.*

Hume, Robert Ernest. *The Thirteen Principal Upanishads.* Oxford: Oxford University Press, 1958.

Klostermaier, Klaus K. *A Survey of Hinduism,* 2nd ed. Albany, NY: SUNY Press, 1994.

Mascaró, Juan. *The Bhagavad Gita.* Baltimore: Penguin Books, 1966.

Mascaró, Juan. *The Upanishads* (selections). Baltimore: Penguin Books, 1965.

Navaratnam, K. *Studies in Hinduism*. Jaffna: M. Navaratnam, 1963.

Panikkar, Raimundo. *The Vedic Experience*. Delhi: Motilal Banarsidass, 1989.

Radhakrishnan, S. *The Hindu View of Life*. New York: Macmillan Publishing, 1975.

Rice, Edward. *Eastern Definitions: A Short Encyclopedia of Religions of the Orient*. Garden City, NY: Doubleday (Anchor Books), 1980.

Ten Questions People Ask About Hinduism…and Ten Terrific answers. Access at www.himalayanacademy.com/basics

Buddhism

http://www.belief.net.com\ (click on Buddhism)

http://www.Asiasource.org (click on Buddhism)

http://www.dharmanet.org/infoweb.html (list of Buddhist organizations and temples around the country, state by state)

Fields. R. *How The Swans Came To The Lake: A Narrative History Of Buddhism In America*. Boston: Shambhala, 1992.

Gehlek, Nawang. *Good Life, Good Death*. Riverhead/ Penguin/Putnam Inc., 2001.

Tricycle: The Buddhist Review. View at http://www.tricycle.com

Judaism

http://jewfaq.org

http://www.jewishlights.com (Resource for Jewish publications)

Gillman, Neil. *The Jewish Approach to God: A Brief Introduction for Christians*. Woodstock, VT: Jewish Lights, 2004.

Kula, Irwin and Vanessa Ochs. *The Book of Jewish Sacred Practices*. Woodstock, VT: Jewish Lights, 2001.

Kushner, Lawrence. *Jewish Spirituality: A Brief Introduction for Christians*. Woodstock, VT: Jewish Lights, 2001.

Christianity

Lewis, C. S. *Mere Christianity*. San Francisco: Harper San Francisco, 2001.

Hinckley, Karen. *A Compact Guide to the Christian Life*. Colorado Springs: Navpress, 1989.

Webb, Jeffrey. *The Complete Idiot's Guide to Christianity* (2nd Edition). New York: Alpha Books, 2004.

Islam

http://www.Islamicity.com

http://www.islam-guide.com (Site includes the book *A Brief Illustrated Guide to Understanding Islam*)

Abd Al-Ati, Hammudah. *Islam in Focus*. Beltsville, MD: Amana Publications, 1997.

Abd Al-Ati, Hammudah. *The Family Structure in Islam*. New Delhi: Islamic Book Service, 1977.

A'la Mauduti, Abul. *Towards Understanding Islam*. Lahore: Idara Tarjuman-ul-Quran, 1990.

Al-Ghazali, Abu Hamid and T.J. Winter. *The Remembrance of Death and the Afterlife*. Islamic Text Society, 1995.

Armstrong, Karen. *Islam: A Short History*. Modern Library, 2000.

Aswad, B.C. and B. Bilge, eds. *Family and Gender Among American Muslims*. Philadelphia: Temple University Press, 1996.

Hodge, David R. "Social Work and the House of Islam: Orienting Practitioners to the Beliefs and Values of Muslims in the United States." *Social Work,* 50,2: 162-173.

Lings, Martin. *Muhammad*. Rochester: Inner Traditions, 1983.

Rahman, Fazlur. *Health and Medicine in the Islamic Tradition*. Kazi Publications, 1998.

Smith, J. I. *Islam in America*. New York: Columbia University press, 1999.

Wilcox, Lynn. *Women and the Holy Qur'an*. M.T.O. Shahmaghsoudi, 1998.

The Islamic Circle of North America, 166-26 89th Ave., Jamaica, NY 11432; 1-800-662-ISLAM.

Appendix II

Resources for Crime Victims

General Resources

National Association of Crime Victim Compensation Boards
www.nacvcb.org
P. O. Box 16003, Alexandria, VA 22302
703-313-9500

National Center for Victims of Crime (NCVC)
www.ncvc.org
2000 M Street NW #480, Washington, D.C. 20036
800-FYI-CALL/202-467-8700 • 202-467-8701 (fax)

National Crime Prevention Council
www.ncpc.org
1000 Connecticut Ave, NW, 13th Floor, Washington, D.C. 20036
202-466-6272 • 202-296-1356 (fax)

National Organization for Victim Assistance (NOVA)
www.try-nova.org
1730 Park Road NW, Washington, D.C. 20010
202-232-6682 • 202-462-2255 (fax)

National Victims Constitutional Amendment Network (NVCAN)
www.ncvan.org
789 Sherman Street, suite 670, Denver, CO 80203
303-832-1522 • 303-861-1265 (fax)

Office for Victims of Crime, U.S. Department of Justice
www.ojp.usdoj.gov/ovc/
810 Seventh Street NW, Washington, D.C. 20531
202-307-5983 • 202-305-2446 (fax)

Office for Victims of Crime Resource Center
www.ojp.usdoj.gov/ovc/ovcres
Box 6000, Rockville, MD 20849-6000
1-800-851-3420

Trauma Counseling Resources

American Psychological Association
www.apa.org
750 First Street NE, Washington, D.C. 22002-4242
800-374-2721• 202-336-5800

Anxiety Disorders Association of America
11900 Parklawn Dr., Suite 100
Rockville, MD 20852-2624

Association of Traumatic Stress Specialists
www.atts-hq.com
PO Box 2747, Georgetown, TX 78627
512-868-3677

The International Society for Traumatic Stress Studies
http://www.istss.org
60 Revere Drive, Suite 500, Northbrook, IL 60062
847-480-9028 • 847-480-9282

National Anxiety Foundation
3135 Custer Drive
Lexington, KY 40517-4001
606-272-7166

National Center for PTSD Web Site
www.ncptsd.org

National Institute for Mental Health
www.nimh.nih.gov
6001 Executive Blvd #8184, MSC, Bethesda, MD 20892
301-443-4513 • 301-443-4279 (fax)

National Mental Health Association
www.nmha.org
1021 Prince Street, Alexandria, VA 22314-2971
800-969-NMHA/703-684-7722

Sidran Institute
www.Sidran.org
Help Desk
200 E. Joppa Rd., Ste. 207, Baltimore, MD 21286
410-825-8888

Journals
- Journal of Traumatic Stress
- Journal of Trauma Practice
- Death Studies
- Muslim Journal of Mental Health

Legal Resources

American Trial Lawyers Association
www.atlanet.org
1050 31st Street NW, Washington, D.C. 20007
800-424-2725

National Crime Victim Bar Association
www.ncvc.org
2000 M Street NW #480, Washington, D.C. 20036
202-467-8753 • 202-467-8701 (fax)

National District Attorneys Association
www.nada.org
99 Canal Center Plaza, Suite 510, Alexandria, VA 22314-1588
843-792-2942 • 843-792-3388 (fax)

Trial Lawyers for Public Justice
www.tlpj.org
1717 Massachusetts Avenue # 800, Washington, D.C. 20036
202-797-8600 • 202-232-7203 (fax)

Victim's Assistance Legal Organization (VALOR)
www.valor-national.org
8180 Greensboro Drive, #1070, McLean, VA 22102-3823
703-748-0811 • 703-356-5085 (fax)

Medical Resources

American College of Emergency Physicians
www.acep.org
1125 Executive Circle, Irving, TX 75038
800-798-1822

American Trauma Society
www.amtrauma.org
8903 Presidential Pkwy, Suite 512, Upper Marlborough, MD 20772
1-800-556-7890

Brain Injury Association
www.biausa.org
105 N. Alfred St., Alexandria, VA 22314
800-444-6443 • 703-236-6001 (fax)

National Head Injury Foundation
www.nhif.org
1776 Massachusetts Avenue NW, #100, Washington, D.C. 20036
1-800-444-6443 • 202-296-8850 (fax)

National Spinal Cord Injury Association
www.spinalcord.org
6701 Democracy Blvd. #300-9, Bethesda, MD 20817
800-962-9629 • 301-588-9414 (fax)

Spirituality Resources

Anti-Violence Partnership of Philadelphia
www.avpphila.org
633 W. Rittenhouse Street, C-12, Philadelphia, PA 19144
215-438-9070

The Maryland Crime Victims' Resource Center, Inc.
National Spirituality and Victim Services Program
www.mdcrimevictims.org
14750 Main Street, suite 1B, Upper Marlboro, MD 20772-3055
301-952-0063 • 301-952-2319 (fax)

Metropolitan Interdenominational Church
SLCrawford@Metropolitanfrc.com
2128 11th Avenue, North, Nashville, TN 37208
615-277-1771

The Sidran Institute
www.sidran.org
200 E. Joppa Road, Ste. 207, Baltimore, MD 21286
410-825-8888

The St. Paul Area Council of Churches
www.spacc.org
1671 Summit Ave., St. Paul, MN 55105
651-646-8805

STAND! Against Domestic Violence
www.standagainstdv.org
12230 San Pablo Ave., Richmond, CA 94805
510-236-8972

University-Based Resources

Center for Victim Studies
California State University-Fresno
www.csufresno.edu
2225 East San Ramon Avenue, Fresno, CA 93740-0104
859-278-4021 • 859-244-8001 (fax)

Crime Victim Study Center
www.newhaven.edu
University of New Haven, 300 Orange Street, West Haven, CT 06516

Joint Center on Violence and Victim Studies
Washburn University and California State University-Fresno
www.washburn.edu/ce/jcvvs
1700 SW College Ave., Topeka, KS 66621
785-231-1010, ext. 1242 • 785-231-1028 (fax)

National Crime Victim's Research and Treatment Center
http://www.musc.edu/cvc/
Department of Psychiatry and Behavioral Sciences
Medical University of South Carolina
165 Cannon Street, PO Box 250852, Charleston, SC 29425
843-792-2945 • 843-792-3388 (fax)

Victims and the Media Resources
www.msu.edu
Michigan State University
School of Journalism
East Lansing, MI 48824-1212
517-353-6430 • 517-336-1244 (fax)

Homicide and Drunk Driving Resources

Association for Death Education and Counseling (ADEC)
www.adec.org
342 North Main Street, West Hartford, CT 06117-2507
860-586-7503 • 860-586-7550 (fax)

Center for Loss and Life Transition
www.centerforloss.com
3735 Broken Bow Road, Ft. Collins, CO 80526
970-226-6050 • 970-226-6051 (fax)

Compassionate Friends
www.compassionatefreinds.com
P.O. Box 3696, Oakbrook, IL 60522-3696
708-990-0010

Compassion Books, Inc.
www.compassionbooks.com
7036 State Hwy. 80 South, Burnsville, NC 28714
828-675-5909 • 828-675-9687 (fax)

Concerns of Police Survivors (COPS)
www.nationalcops.org
P.O. Box 3199, South Highway Five, Camdenton, MO 65020
573-346-4911 • 573-346-1414 (fax)

Million Moms March United with the Brady Campaign (Gunshot Survivors)
www.millionmommarch.com
1225 Eye St. NW, Suite 1100, Washington, D.C. 20005
888-989-6667

Mothers Against Drunk Driving (MADD)
www.madd.org
511 E. John Carpenter Fwy. #700, Irving, TX 75062
1-800-438-6233

National Clearinghouse for Alcohol and Drug Information
www.health.org
11426-28 Rockville Pike, Suite 200, Rockville, MD 20852
1-800-729-6686

National Coalition of Homicide Survivors
www.mvictims.org
Pima County Attorneys Office
32 N. Stone, 11th Floor, Tucson, AX 85701
520-740-5729 • 520-740-5642 (fax)

National Commission Against Drunk Driving
www.ncadd.org
1900 L Street, N.W., Suite 705, Washington, D.C. 20036
202-452-6004 • 202-223-7012 (fax)

National Funeral Directors Association
www.nfda.org
13625 Bishops Drive, Brookfield, WI 53005
800-228-6322 • 262-789-6977 (fax)

Parents of Murdered Children
www.pomc.com
100 E. 8th Street, B-41, Cincinnati, OH 45202
888-818-7662 • 513-345-4489 (fax)

Tragedy Assistance Program for Survivors (TAPS)
(Military Deaths)
www.taps.org
2001 S Street NW #300, Washington, D.C. 20009
1-800-959-8277 • 202-639-5312 (fax)

Women's Abuse (Rape, Domestic Violence) Resources

American Bar Association Commission on Domestic Violence
www.abanet.org/domviol/about
740 15th Street NW, 9th Floor, Washington, D.C. 20005-1022

Domestic Abuse Intervention Project (DAIP)
www.vaw.umn.edu
206 W. Fourth St., Room 201, Duluth, MN 55806
218-722-2781 or 218-722-4134 • 218-722-1545 (fax

Domestic Violence Project of the American Academy of Facial Plastic and Reconstructive Surgery
www.aafprs.org
310 S. Henry Street, Alexandria, VA 22314
703-299-9291, 703-299-8898 (fax)

FaithTrust Institute
National Clearinghouse on Religion and Abuse
www.cpsdv.org
2400 N. 45th Street, Suite 10, Seattle, WA 98103
206-634-1903 • 206-634-0115 (fax)

Family Violence Prevention Fund
www.fvpf.org
383 Rhode Island St., Suite 304, San Francisco, CA 94103
888-792-2873/415-252-8990, 415-252-8991 (fax)

Islamic Social Services Association (ISSA)
1030 E. Baseline Road, Suite 105, PMB 955
Tempe, AZ 85283-1314
Phone: (888) 532-7057
Email: info@issausa.org
Website: www. issausa.org

Jewish Women International
http://www.jewishwomen.org (Resource to help Jewish women who are victims of violence.)

Karamah: Muslim Women Layers for Human Rights
1420 16th Street, NW, Washington, DC 20036
Phone: (202) 234-7302 • Fax: (202) 234-7304
Email: karamah@karamah.org • Website: www.karamah.org

Stop Violence Against Indian Women Technical Assistance Project
202 East Superior Street, Duluth, MN 55802
218-722-2781 or 1-888-305-1650 • 218-722-5775 (fax)

National Clearinghouse for the Defense of Battered Women
www.aclu.org
125 South 9th Street, Suite 302, Philadelphia, PA 19107
800-903-0111 ext. 3 • 215-351-0779 (fax)

National Clearinghouse on Marital and Date Rape
www.ncmdr.org
2325 Oak Street, Berkeley, CA 94708
510-524-1582

National Coalition Against Domestic Violence
www.ncadv.org
18749/1201 Colfax Ave., Suite 385, Denver, CO 80209
303-839-1852 • 303-831-9251 (fax)

National Network to End Domestic Violence
www.ndvh.org
660 Pennsylvania Avenue, SE, Suite 303, Washington, WA 20003
202-543-5566

National Resource Center on Domestic Violence
6400 Flank Dr., Suite 1300, Harrisburg, PA 17112-2778
800-537-2238 • 717-545-9456 (fax)

Peaceful Families Project
P.O. Box 771
Great Falls, VA 22066
Phone: (703) 474-6870
Email: info@peacefulfamilies.org
Website: www.peacefulfamilies.org

Resource Center on Domestic Violence, National Council of Juvenile and Family Court Judges

Family Violence Project
P.O. Box 8970, Reno, NV 89507
702-784-6012 • 800-527-3223

Violence Against Women's Office (VAWO)

www.usdoj.gov/vawo
810 7th Street NW, Washington, D.C. 20531
202-307-6026 • 202-307-3911 (fax)

Journals
- *Aggression and Violent Behavior*
- *Journal of Emotional Abuse*
- *Journal of Family Violence*
- *Journal of Interpersonal Violence*
- *Journal of Traumatic Stress*
- *Violence Against Women*

Women's Abuse Hotlines

Battered Women's Justice Project
800-903-0111

National Domestic Violence Hotline

www.ndhvh.org
3616 Far West Blvd., Suite 101-297, Austin, TX 78731
800-799-SAFE (7233) (hotline)
800-787-3224 (TDD)
512-453-8117 (administration)

Staffed 24 hours a day by trained counselors who can provide crisis assistance and information about shelters, legal advocacy, health care centers, and counseling.

RAINN Hotline
www.rainn.org
1-800-656-HOPE
202-544-3556 (Fax)

The Rape, Abuse, Incest National Network will automatically transfers victims to the rape crisis center nearest them, anywhere in the nation. It can be used if people cannot find a domestic violence shelter.

Child Abuse Resources

American Bar Association Center on Children and the Law
www.abanet.org
1800 M Street NW, Suite 200-S, Washington, DC 20036
202-331-2250

American Civil Liberties Union (ACLU):
Children's Rights Project
www.aclu.org
132 W. 43rd St., New York, NY 10036
212-229-0540 • 212-229-0749 (fax)

American Humane Association: American Association
for Protecting Children (AAPC)
www.americanhumane.org
63 Inverness Dr. East, Englewood, CO 80112-5117
800-227-4645 • 303-792-5333 (fax)

American Professional Society on the Abuse
of Children (APSAC)
www.aapasac.org
332 S. Michigan Ave. Suite 1600, Chicago, IL 60604
312-554-0166 • 312-554-0919 (fax)

Childhelp USA
www.childhelpusa.org
15757 North 78th Street, Scottsdale, AZ 85260
800-4-A-CHILD/480-922-7061 • 480-922-7061 (fax)

Child Welfare League of America (CWLA)
www.cwla.org
440 First St. NW, Suite 310, Washington, DC 20001-2085
202-638-2952

Family Resource Coalition
www.frca.org
20 N. Wacker Dr., Ste. 1100, Chicago, IL 60606
312-338-0900 • 312-338-1522 (fax)

Family Violence and Sexual Assault Institute
www.fvsai.org
6160 Cornerstone Court East, San Diego, CA 92121

Family Violence Prevention Fund
www.fvpf.org
383 Rhode Island St., Suite 304, San Francisco, CA 94103
415-252-8900 • 415-252-8991(fax)

Father Flanagan's Boys Home (Boys Town)
www.azaz.essortment.com/boystown
14100 Crawford St., Boys Town, NE 68010
402-498-1301

National Center for Missing and Exploited Children
www.missingkids.com
Charles B. Wang International Children's Building
699 Prince Street, Arlington, VA 22314-3175
800-826-7653 • 703-274-3900

National Center for Prosecution of Child Abuse: American Prosecutors Research Institute
www.ndaa.org/apri
99 Canal Center Plaza, Suite 510, Alexandria, VA 22314
703-739-0321

National Center on Child Abuse and Neglect (NCCAN)
www.calib.com/nccan
U.S. Department of Health and Human Services
P.O. Box 1182, Washington, DC 20013
800-394-3366 • 703-385-7565

National Children's Alliance
www.nca-online.org
1612 K Street, NW, Suite 500, Washington, D.C. 20006
202-452-6001 • 202-452-6002 (fax)

National Committee to Prevent Child Abuse (NCPCA)
www.casanet.org/library/abuse/ncpca
332 S. Michigan Ave., Suite 1600, Chicago, IL 60604
312-663-3520

PACER Center
www.pacer.org
8161 Normandale Blvd., Minneapolis, MN 55437
952-838-9000 • 952-838-0199 (fax)

VOICES in Action, Inc. (Victims of Incest Can Emerge Survivors)
www.voices-action.org
P.O. Box 148309, Chicago, IL 60614
800-7VO-ICE8 / 773-327-1500

Hotlines
- Father Flanagan's Boys Home 800-448-3000

- National Child Abuse Hotline 800-422-4453 or
  800-4-A-Child

Journals
- *Aggressions and Violent Behavior*
- *Child Abuse & Neglect*
- *Journal of Child Sexual Abuse*
- *Journal of Emotional Abuse*
- *Journal of Family Violence*
- *Journal of Interpersonal Violence*

Elder Abuse Resources

American Association of Retired Persons
www.aarp.org
Criminal Justice Services
601 E. Street, NW, Washington, DC 20049
(202) 434-2222

Elder Care Locator
(to locate the nearest Adult Protective Services Agency)
1-800-677-1116

National Center on Elder Abuse
www.elderabusecenter.org
1201 15th St., NW, Suite 350, Washington, DC 20005
(202) 682-0100

Appendix III

Books and DVDs on Women's & Children's Victimization Issues and Spirituality

Unless otherwise noted, the materials reviewed below are available from the *FaithTrust Institute,* a national organization headquartered in Seattle, Washington, which has been serving religious and community groups throughout the world since 1977. *FaithTrust Institute* works with many cultures, including Asian and Pacific Islander, African American, Latino/a, and Indigenous. A diverse range of faith communities – including Jewish, Roman Catholic Christian, Protestant Christian, Buddhist, Muslim, and Indigenous – utilize their resources.

FaithTrust Institute envisions a world where religious institutions create a climate in which abuse is not tolerated. Faith communities become sanctuaries of safety, worthy of our trust, and all of us experience justice and healing in our communities.

The staff at *FaithTrust Institute* is available for training seminars and keynote presentations in your area. Subjects include religious aspects of:

- Domestic violence
- Child abuse
- Sexual violence
- Sexual abuse by clergy

FaithTrust Institute
www.faithtrustinstitute.org
To place orders, order online or call:
1-877-860-2255 • 1-206-634-0055

Domestic Violence Multi-Faith Resources

Broken Vows: Religious Perspectives on Domestic Violence (DVD)

Introduced by a Christian pastor and Jewish rabbi, this color video presents the stories of six battered women – Jewish, Roman Catholic Christian, and Protestant Christian. One woman is a Caucasian professor at a Christian Evangelical college; one was an African-American protestant pastor's wife; one is a Hispanic Catholic; one is a Native American Christian, one is Jewish, and one is Caucasian Protestant. They explain their struggle to remain faithful to their spiritual heritage and, as the same time, learn how to take a stand against what is clearly wrong. Their stories are interspersed with Catholic and Protestant pastors and rabbis who understand that their faiths do not condone violence and offer support to women who experience it. A key point echoed by several of the faith leaders is that violence breaks the covenant of marriage long before separation or divorce is considered.

Family Violence and Religion: An Interfaith Resource Guide
Compiled by the Staff of Volcano Press

This publication is more an academic resource than a practical tool for victims. The book's value lies in its diversity, with sections on alcohol abuse and domestic violence, domestic violence in rural areas, Asian-American patriarchies, an African-American perspective on domestic violence, cultural issues for Hispanic-American battered women, elderly battered women, and Christian and Jewish perspectives on abuse. One of the most valuable sections of the book for Jews and Christians is a three-page chapter titled "The Rod of Guidance" which explains that, in Hebrew, the "rod" was used by shepherds to care for and guide the sheep – never to hit them. It lists various ways the rod was used to protect the sheep from harm.

Forgiveness and Abuse: Jewish and Christian Reflections
Edited by Rev. Dr. Marie Fortune and Dr. Joretta Marshall

This book looks deeply and thoroughly into the meaning of forgiveness and what it requires. It explores theological, psychological, and ethical aspects of forgiveness in the Jewish and Christian traditions within the context of abuse. Only 152 pages long, this book will educate the seriously faithful victims of violence about their faith tradition's expectations surrounding the difficult topic of forgiveness.

Love: All that and More (DVD)

This product is a set of three videos and a six-session 50-minute each curriculum designed to inform high school and college age youth about what makes healthy relationships. To increase their awareness about abuse, and to motivate them to seek relationships based on equality and mutual respect.

Pastoral Care for Domestic Violence: Case Studies for Clergy (DVD)

An important training DVD for Christian and Jewish clergy. This multifaith series of role plays demonstrates Catholic, Protestant and Jewish clergy effectively addressing common religious issues raised by victims, survivors and abusers in situations of domestic violence. This comprehensive training package is designed to be used for audiences who have an understanding of the religious aspects of domestic violence (best used subsequent to *Broken Vows*). Also ideal for use in theological education.

Walking Together: Working with Women from Diverse Religious and Spiritual Traditions. A Guide for Domestic Violence Advocates.
Edited by Jean Anton

An important anthology for domestic violence advocates. Includes information about American Indian/Alaskan Native Spirituality, Buddhism, Catholicism, Hinduism, Islam, Judaism and Protestantism.

What Every Congregation Needs to Know about Domestic Violence

This brochure for Christian and Jewish faith communities, battered women's programs, and human service providers answers basic questions about domestic violence and explains what church and synagogue members can do individually and collectively to address it in their congregations. It is available in English, Chinese, Korean, Laotian, Spanish, and Vietnamese.

Jewish Resources

A Journey Towards Freedom: A Haggadah for Women Who Have Experienced Domestic Violence

This book transforms the traditional Passover Seder into a special service that addresses the oppression and liberation of women journeying from abuse to safety. It is an excellent resource to supplement the Passover Haggadah for congregations and domestic violence programs that serve Jewish women.

To Save a Life: Ending Domestic Violence in Jewish Families (DVD)

The long tradition of valuing family life in Judaism makes it difficult to believe that the percentage of Jewish women who are abused is as high as in other populations. Designed specifically for abused Jewish women, this 35-minute color video features several Jewish women who share their abuse experiences (one of them, Jae, is also in *Broken Vows*, mentioned above). Five rabbis appear in the video, each one emphasizing that a Jew's primary obligation is to preserve life, including the victim's own life and the lives of her children (*Whoever saves a single life has saved a entire universe* - Talmud.) The video provides information about abuse in Jewish families and a comprehensive discussion of theological issues such as *shalom bayit* (household harmony), forgiveness and atonement. It points out that it is not only the wife's responsibility to maintain household harmony, but the husband's as well. It also includes information about the effects of domestic violence on children.

You Are Not Alone: Solace and Inspiration for Domestic Violence Survivors Based on Jewish Wisdom **By Toby Landesman**

Domestic violence occurs within all streams of Judaism: Conservative, Orthodox, Reconstructionist, Reform, Renewal, and among Jews who do not identify with any particular Movement. For Jewish domestic violence victims and the professionals who help them, this book informs about the problem and explains what Judaism says about it. A very useful Appendix informs victims and faith leaders about how to develop a Safety Plan, people and places that can help, and national hotlines, agencies, and websites.

Christian Resources

Circles of Healing

Designed to complement *Wings Like a Dove*, this is a 3-session support group curriculum for abused Christian women. Each session includes worship materials, scripture reflections, discussion questions, and closing prayers.

Domestic Violence: What Churches Can Do (DVD)

This 20-minute color video is an edited version of *Broken Vows* and includes worship materials, background information on domestic violence, discussion questions, and practical steps Christian congregations can take to prevent domestic violence. The materials are sufficient for a one-hour presentation.

God's Reconciling Love: A Pastor's Handbook on Domestic Violence
By Nancy A. Murphy, M.A.

In his foreword, Dr. Dan Allender, President of Mars Hill Graduate School, points out that "this well-designed manual, written by a wise and amazing woman, will not only answer the majority of questions Christian pastors ask about domestic violence, but embolden them to make the path safe for both victim and perpetrator." Short and very readable (less than 100 pages), the book informs about domestic violence but also presents pastors' perspectives and presents workable solutions. One of the most useful sections of the book is "One Couple's Story" by Rev. Dr. Randy Bridges, a Baptist pastor who recounts his experience of learning to deal appropriately with domestic violence in his congregation. It also includes a fine resource list at the back.

Keeping the Faith: Guidance for Christian Women Facing Abuse
By Rev. Dr. Marie M. Fortune

This classic, available in English, Korean, and Spanish, was written in response to Marie Fortune's work with women being abused in Christian homes and women in shelters. She listened to women who had been ostracized by their churches and counseled by their pastors to go home and be a better Christian wife. She also talked with women who found caring support from their pastors and churches. One by one, the book responds to questions Christian women ask about domestic violence. From the Psalms through the Gospels through the letters of Paul, distortions and misconceptions about scriptures sometimes used to excuse abuse are corrected.

Opening the Door: A Pastor's Guide to Addressing Domestic Violence in Premarital Counseling. **By Rev. Susan Yarrow Morris in collaboration with Jean Anton.**

A critical new interdenominational resource for Christian pastors and counselors seeking to prevent domestic violence.

Wings Like a Dove: Healing for the Abused Christian Woman (DVD)

See the description of *Broken Vows* in the **Multi-Faith Resources** section above. *Wings Like a Dove* includes only the Christian survivor and pastor segments and is intended for Christian audiences.

Change from Within: Diverse Perspectives on Domestic Violence in Muslim Communities. **Edited by Maha B. Alkhateeb and Salma Elkadi Abugideiri**

To date, domestic violence in Muslim communities has received little attention. *Change From Within* is one of the first edited volumes to focus on domestic violence in Muslim families. Bringing the experiences of diverse domestic violence advocates to the table, voices in the text include religious leaders, services providers, and researchers from multiple disciplines. Four survivors also share their stories, illustrating some of the challenges they faced, as well as their paths to healing. This volume illuminates unique domestic violence issues that Muslims face, and emphasizes Islam's intolerance to abuse.

Garments for One Another: Ending Domestic Violence in Muslim Families (DVD)

An important new resource for mosques, religious leaders, social workers, community groups and shelter staff who offer help to Muslim women who currently experience violence in the home. This complete package offers solutions to prevent future violence within the context of the Islamic faith. Includes interviews with survivors, religious leaders, and community advocates.

What Islam Says About Domestic Violence
By Zainab Alwani and Salma Abugideiri

This practical guide for helping Muslim victims of domestic violence is a valuable resource for shelters, Imams, and others who serve Muslim victims. It is also recommended for *all* those who serve these victims in order to dismiss rampant myths about violence among Muslims. In Islam, spouses are inherently equal. Cultural groups who proclaim inequality are speaking more from a cultural than spiritual perspective. The foundation of Islamic marriage is described in the Qur'an: *And among His signs is this: that He created for you mates from among yourselves that you may dwell in tranquility with them, and He has put love and mercy between your (hearts)* (30:21). Because Islam and Middle Eastern culture are relatively unfamiliar to many in this country, this book was designed offer information and answers to frequently asked questions. Copies are available from Foundation for Appropriate and Immediate Temporary Help, 500 Grove Street, Ste. 210, Herndon, VA 20172. www.faithus.org. E-mail info@faithus.org.

Child Abuse Multi-Faith Resources

Hear Their Cries (DVD)

This 48-minute, color video, introduced by a Christian pastor and a rabbi, defines physical, sexual, and emotional abuse and includes the stories of numerous adult survivors of child abuse. Pastors and rabbis discuss theological issues such as forgiveness and confidentiality within the context of child abuse. They point out that the goal of any faith community should be to (1) protect the child, (2) stop the abuse, and (3) attempt to reunite the family although that may not be possible. Guidelines are given about how to respond when a child discloses abuse. While a very valuable tool for congregations, the inclusion of material on the long-term emotional consequences of spanking that does not leave marks would make it stronger.

The Healing Years: A Documentary About Surviving Incest and Child Sexual Abuse (DVD)

This 52-minute, color video profiles the painful journey of three women as they seek healing and recovery from incest as children. *Marilyn Van Derbur*, a former Miss America opens the video by revealing that she and her three sisters survived the incest of their father, but she eventually became physically paralyzed as a means of psychologically coping between the ages of 45 and 51. She says, *"I believed I was bad and dirty for 53 years… It just underscores what happens in a child's mind when her young body is pried open and violated. It is our belief systems that are shattered. It isn't just the physical invasion of our bodies. It's the trauma that it does to our entire belief system… You are not allowed to hate your violator – because he's your father."*

Janice Mirikitani, wife of the pastor of Glide Memorial Methodist Church in San Francisco, speaks of her long-term substance abuse as a means of escaping the pain of incest by her stepfather from the time she was 5 until she was 16. Barbara Hamilton, at age 79, continues to work on her incest issues from her father, as do her children whom he also abused. She finally broke the silence, ending three generations of incest.

The video shows how Janice Mirikitani now facilitates incest and substance abuse recovery groups at her church where 90% of female substance abusers are also incest survivors.

What You Need to Know if a Child is Being Abused or Neglected

This brochure for Christian and Jewish faith communities, available in English, Korean, and Spanish, answers basic questions about child abuse and neglect and explains what church and synagogue members can do individually and collectively to address it in their congregations.

Jewish Resources

Shine the Light: Sexual Abuse and Healing in the Jewish Community **By Rachel Lev**

This book, published in 2003, was written by a woman who is an incest survivor and a therapist. She tells the story of numerous Jewish incest survivors as they reflect on their personal relationships with the Jewish community. In some cases it discouraged denial; in others it was a source of healing. She reveals Judaism to be rich in resources for healing as she explores Jewish law, tradition, and rituals including the thoughts of rabbis and Jewish community leaders.

Christian Resources

Bless Our Children: Preventing Sexual Abuse (DVD)

This 40-minute, color video is the story of how a Christian church struggled with the decision about introducing a curriculum to prevent sexual abuse. Some opposed it because they didn't think it happened in their congregation. Others didn't want to upset children with the topic. Still others didn't want to interrupt regular programming to address it. However, they eventually reviewed a children's Sunday School curriculum published by the United church Press (see below) and realized that it was very tastefully done and interwoven around traditional Bible stories. Actual classroom segments are included. In the end, they know what to do when a child discloses that she is being fondled by a tutor. This video could be very effective for clergy continuing education or seminary classes.

Preventing Child Sexual Abuse Program (Sunday School Curriculum) **Published by The United Church Press**

Separate curricula are available for three age groups.

Sexual Abuse of Adult Women by Clergy

It is not uncommon for clergy to misuse their power and engage congregants in sexual relationships. While these relationships do not represent a breaking of the law, as do the forms of abuse noted above, they represent clear ethical violations. Obtaining justice is a prerequisite to healing. When exploitation occurs, the following materials establish elements for achieving justice: (1) victim truth-telling, (2) acknowledgment of the violation by the clergy and the faith community, (3) compassion for the victim, (4) protection of the vulnerable, (5) accountability of the clergy abuser, and (6) vindication. Basic components of policies and procedures to handle these situations are recommended for churches and synagogues.

Book:

- *Is Nothing Sacred?* The Story of a Pastor, the Women He Sexually Abused, and the Congregation He Nearly Destroyed by Marie M. Fortune.

Videos:

- *A Sacred Trust: Boundary Issues for Clergy and Spiritual Teachers* includes four 22-minute videos with a curriculum. It includes specific Appendices on boundary issues for African American communities, Asian and Pacific Islander communities, Jewish communities, Latina and Latino communities, and Lesbian/Gay/Bisexual and Transgendered clergy or spiritual teachers. Meditations and prayers are included in the Buddhist, Jewish, and Christian traditions.

- *Not in My Church*, a 45-minutes color video for Christian audiences.

- *Not in My Congregation*, a 48-minute color video for Jewish audiences.

- *Once You Cross the Line*, a 50-minute, six-segment video on preventing clergy misconduct and sexual abuse in ministerial relationships.

Appendix iv

How to Develop an Interfaith Group:
The Experience of Daughters of Abraham
(Jewish, Christian, and Muslim women)

Be patient.

It takes time to build trust, even among sub-groups of one faith or among members of any one group. No matter how open-minded you are, you (yes, even you) have some stereotypical ideas

Begin with a small group of representatives of the three faiths. In starting the original Daughters of Abraham, the wife of a Christian minister asked her husband to approach a rabbi and an imam he knew to see if they would invite 5 or 6 women their faiths to meet with 5 or 6 Christian women to explore starting a group. This step may not be necessary if a handful of women from the three faiths are already friends.

These women do not need to be faith leaders, but should be interested in improving inter-faith relationships and be comfortable sharing their own faith pilgrimage without feeling a need to proselytize others. This initial group will probably want to meet together for several months to move beyond tolerance to mutual respect and appreciation of each other before attempting to reach out to the larger community. Early meetings might offer the opportunity for the women to share basic information about their faith, correct myths or misunderstandings, and identify common themes. We have found that it works best just to announce a discussion topic and invite everyone to share. At the end of each gathering, a discussion topic can be chosen for the next gathering. Prepared "presentations" are not very successful because not enough time is generally available for relationship building and discussion.

Decide what you want to accomplish.

Our goal was not to develop a short-term educational dialogue but to provide a warm and inviting setting for the building of long-term, enduring relationships. In other words, we wanted to grow in respect and love for each other. While women may come and go from the group when they choose, we aim to be a welcoming family where many of us remain together for years. From time to time, we have to actively seek out women from a particular faith to keep the balance at our meetings fairly even, but generally the attitude is "come as long as you find it meaningful."

When you are ready to formalize your group, you may want to develop a statement of purpose or mission statement. The one we chose is:

Daughters of Abraham is a group formed by women of three faiths – Judaism, Christianity, and Islam – to enhance understanding of our spiritual and cultural similarities. At our monthly meetings, we share ideas and values to promote good welfare among the communities.

Remember that an interfaith program is not a melting pot program.

A Daughters of Abraham group is more like a mosaic than a melting pot. It is not realistic to seek to reduce each faith to a common denominator. However, it is reasonable to focus on multiple manifestations and expressions of a common theme such as peace or anti-violence. Never expect all groups to pray the same way. A successful group acknowledges differences but seeks to identify commonalities.

It is important that differences of opinion be shared honestly but respectfully. Secrets or gossip outside the group has rarely been a problem, but when it has been we have tried to address the concern with the whole group as soon as possible.

Identify a strong communicator, but diversify leadership.

One person must be willing to maintain a current and accurate e-mail and snail mail list of all those who want to be informed of gatherings of the group. This list should be passed around at each gathering to assure that addresses, phone numbers, and e-mail address are current, and that new group members can sign up. Remember that not everyone uses the Internet, so those who prefer to be notified by mail or phone should be.

This great communicator, however, is not necessarily the group facilitator. We have found it best to rotate facilitators, depending on the meeting site. We have intentionally NOT elected officers because we want the feel to be circular and democratic rather than vertical and structured

Meet at different places.

The sites of meetings should rotate among the faiths, perhaps at a church one time and a synagogue, temple, or mosque the next. The host "site" may select a discussion facilitator from their own membership. We enjoy having food at our gatherings, and the host site prepares the refreshments. That way, each faith group only furnishes refreshments 3 times a year, excluding Ramadan month when we join our Muslim sisters in fasting.

We have regular monthly gatherings from September through May, and have a couple of special activities in the summer. One is a pot-luck supper where spouses join us for a wonderful meal. This has become so popular that we are considering having one more than once a year. We also have a book review retreat day each summer at the home of one of the group members. Books addressed have included *The Secret Life of Bees, Abraham: A Journey to the Heart of three Faiths, The Kite Runner, The Faith Club, Pretty Birds,* and *The Lemon Tree.*

Make the setting symbolic of your intent.

We have our gatherings in a circular setting, usually with tables so notes can be taken by those who enjoy that. The host site sometimes uses colorful table cloths or table decorations representing their own faith symbols or holidays. Sometimes the tables are plain. The circular setting assures that no one is "up front" and that the discussion facilitator is on equal plane with everyone else.

Be considerate of holy days and times.

Muslims pray on Fridays at noon. The Jewish Sabbath begins at sundown on Friday and ends at sundown on Saturday. Some Christian denominations worship on Saturday. Jewish Rosh Hashana initiates a 10-day period of reflection in the fall that ends on the Highest Jewish Holy Day, Yom Kippur. Plan meetings and events that do not conflict with these sacred times.

Discuss whatever you want to.

Following are some discussion topics our group has addressed:
- Prayer styles
- Holy Books
- Holidays
- Common Heroes of the Faith
- Basic Beliefs
- Death and Dying Rituals
- Marriage Rituals (We brought our wedding pictures for this discussion.)
- Forgiveness (This meeting discussion followed a meeting in which a Holocaust survivor shared her concentration camp experiences.)
- Modesty
- Concerns about the Next Generation
- Stereotypes and Biases (This gathering included distributing 3 X 5 cards in which each women filled in the blank for "Before joining Daughters of Abraham, I thought Jews…….." This statement was given for Christianity and Islam also. The 4th statement was, "Now I believe that…….." In order to avoid embarrassing anyone, the cards were shuffled and redistributed. Each woman read aloud the card she drew and then shared what she wanted to about whether her experiences was similar to or different from the author of the card.)

We have found that a discussion topic for the next meeting often develops out of the current discussion.

For More Information

If you would like more information about Daughters of Abraham, you may write us at:

Daughters of Abraham
5903 Tiffany Court, Arlington, TX 76016
Phone/FAX: 817-492-9208
E-Mail: janice@jhlord.org
www.jhlord.org/daughtersofabraham

NOTES

Preface, pages xiii-xv

1. This is the subtitle of Diana Eck, *A New Religious America: How a "Christian Country" Has Become the World's Most Religiously Diverse Nation* (New York: HarperCollins, 2002).

2. Population Reference Bureau, Available at http://www.prb.org/countries/UnitedStates.aspx; also http://www.census.gov accessed November 20, 2007.

3. U.S. Department of Justice, Immigration and Naturalization Service, *Legal Immigration Annual Report, Fiscal Year 2001* (Washington, D.C.: Dept. of Homeland Security Immigration Archives, Yearbook of Immigration Statistics, August 2002), p. 1. Available at http://www.dhs.gov/xlibrary/assets/statistics/reports/IMM2001.pdf.

4. Jeffrey S. Passel, Randolph Capps, and Michael E. Fix, "Undocumented Immigrants: Facts and Figures." Washington, DC: The Urban Institute, 2004. Available at http://www.urban.org/publications/900898 accessed November 29, 2007.

5. Rakesh Kochar, "Latino Labor Report, First Quarter 2004: Wage Growth Lags Gains in Employment." Washington, D.C.: Pew Hispanic Center, Report released June 21, 2004. Available at http://pewhispanic.org/files/reports/29.1.pdf.

6. Steven A.Camarota, :Immigrants at Mid-Decade: A Snapshot of America's Foreign-Born Population in 2005." Washington, D.C. Center for Immigration Studies Report analyzing Census Bureau data. Report available at http://www.cis.org/topics/currentnumbers.html Also see http://www.census.gov accessed September 15, 2007.

7. Ibid.

8. U.S. Department of Veteran Affairs. Available at http://www.cem.va.gov/cem/hm/hmemb.asp accessed Nobember 29, 2007.

9. Barry Kosmin and Seymour Lachman, (2002) *Top Twenty Religions in the United States*, New York: City University of New York. Available at http://www.adherents.com/rel.USA.htm#religions Accessed December 6, 2007.

10. C. Power (1998, March 16). The new Islam. Newsweek, 34. Available at http://www.islamfortoday.com/historyusa4.htm

11. Barna Research Group, *Crime Victim and Crime Prevention Ministry: A Study of U.S. Churches*, Oxnard, CA: Barna Research Group; ETP, Inc., "The Faith-Community Victim-Services Support Project: A Concept Paper," Submitted to Office for Victims of Crime, December 2001.

Chapter 1, Spiritually Sensitive Caregiving, pages 25-39

1. H. G. Koenig, M. McCullough, and D. B. Larson, *Handbook of Religion and Health* (New York: Oxford University Press, 2001).

2. Ibid.

3. *Everson v. Board of Education*, 330 U.S. 1 (1947). Available at www.oyez.org/oyez/resource/case/114 Accessed May 2, 2004.

4. David Barton, *Original Intent: The Courts, the Constitution & Religion* (Aledo, TX: WallBuilder Press, 2000), 46.

5. *Everson v. Board of Education.*

6. The Associated Press, "AmeriCorps Sponsor Must Stop Funding Catholic Programs, July 7, 2004. Available at http://www.firstamendmentcenter.org/news.aspx?id=13666 accessed November 29, 2007.

7. *Lemon v. Kurtzman*, 403 U.S. 602 (1971). Available at www.oyez.org/oyez/resource/case/207.

8. Anna Greenberg, "Doing Whose Work? Faith-Based Organizations and Government partnerships," in *Who Will Provide? The Changing Role of Religion in American Social Welfare*, ed. Mary Jo Bane, Brent Coffin, and Ronald F. Thiemann (Boulder, CO: Westview Press, 2000).

9. Stephen V. Monsma, *When Sacred and Secular Mix*, 30-31, quoted in Greenberg, Ibid.

10. See *Bradfield v. Roberts*, 175 U.S. 291 (1899) and *Bowen v. Kendrick*,

487.U.S. 589, 609 (1988). Cited in "Participation in Justice Department Programs by Religious Organizations: Providing for Equal Treatment of All Justice Department Program Participants," Final Rule published by the Office of the Attorney General, Justice, in the *Federal Register*, vol. 69, no. 13, January 21, 2004; p. 2836.

11. "Participation in Justice Department Programs by Religious Organizations: Providing for Equal Treatment of All Justice Department Program Participants," Final Rule published by the Office of the Attorney General, Justice, in the *Federal Register*, vol. 69, no. 13, January 21, 2004, p. 2832.

12. H. G. Koenig, *Spirituality in Patient Care* (Philadelphia: Templeton Foundation Press, 2002), 21.

13. D. A. Matthews and C. Clark, *The Faith Factor* (New York: Penguin), 1999.

14. Edward R. Canda and Leola Dyrud Furman, *Spiritual Diversity in Social Work Practice* (New York: The Free Press, 1999), xxiii.

15. Crime Victims Institute, *The Impact of Crime on Victims: Final Report* (Austin, TX: Office of the Attorney General, 1998), 97; Dorothy Mercer, Steven Falkenberg, and Roseanne Lorden, "Spirituality and Drunk Driving Victimization," *MADDvocate* (Winter 1999): 13, 22; C. Roy Woodruff, "New National Survey Affirms Desire for Pastoral Counseling," *Currents* 39, no. 2 (Spring 2001): 21, 22.

16. Canda, *Spiritual Diversity*, 264. Adapted from Edward R. Canda, "A Holistic Approach to Prayer for Social Work Practice," *Social Thought* 16, no. 3 (1990): 3–13.

17. Sherry A. Falsetti, Patricia A. Resick, and Joanne L. Davis, "Changes in Religious Beliefs Following Trauma," *Journal of Traumatic Stress*, 16, no. 4 (August 2003): 391–398.

18. Ibid., 396.

19. Brandon Toropov and Father Luke Buckles, *The Complete Idiot's Guide to World Religions* (New York: Alpha Books, 1997), 21–25.

20. United Church of Canada, *That We May Know Each Other: United Church–Muslim Relations Today* (Toronto: The United Church of Canada, 2004), 47.

21. Federal Bureau of Investigation, *Crime in the United States: Uniform Crime Reports, 2001* (Washington, D.C.: U.S. Department of Justice, Federal Bureau of Investigation, 2002).

22. American-Arab Anti-Discrimination Committee, *ADC Fact Sheet: The Condition of Arab-Americans Post 9/11*, (Washington D.C.: American-Arab Anti-Discrimination Committee, 2002).

23. John M. Buchanan, "Consequences," *Christian Century* (October 16, 2007): 3.

24. Ramdas Lamb, personal communication with the author, August 5, 2002.

25. Ibid.

26. Brian K. Ogawa, *The Color of Justice*, 2nd ed. (Boston: Allyn and Bacon, 1999).

27. For more information go to www.professionalchaplains.org
28. For more information go to www.aapc.org

Chapter 2, Native American Spirituality, pages 41-61

1. Alvin, M. Josephy, *The Indian Heritage of America* (New York: Bantam Books, 1973), 30–46.

2. N. Scott Momaday, *The Way to Rainy Mountain* (Albuquerque: University of New Mexico Press, 2001), 3.

3. M. Gallegos, Interim Director of the Mid-American All-Indian Center in Wichita, Kansas, interview with the author, April 20, 2004.

4. John G. Neihardt, *Black Elk Speaks* (Lincoln: University of Nebraska Press, 1932), 1.

5. Robert M. Utley, *The Lance and the Shield* (New York: Henry Holt, 1993), 281.

6. Ed McGaa (Eagle Man), *Mother Earth Spirituality* (San Francisco: HarperSanFrancisco, 1990), 126.

7. Momaday, *Way to Rainy Mountain*, 4.

8. Neihardt, *Black Elk Speaks*.

9. Vine Deloria, Jr., *God is Red* (Golden, CO: Fulcrum Publishing, 2003), 295.

10. Donald J. Berthrong, *The Southern Cheyennes* (Norman, OK: University of Oklahoma Press, 1979), 50.

11. McGaa, *Mother Earth Spirituality*, 85–96.

12. Ibid., 99–100

13. For more information, see Brown, Joseph, *The Sacred Pipe: Black Elk's Account of the Seven Rites of the Oglala Sioux*, Norman, OK: University of Oklahoma Press, 1953.

14. Bureau of Justice Statistics, *National Crime Victimization Survey* (Washington, D.C.: U.S. Department of Justice, Bureau of Justice Statistics, 1999). For current statistics, access www.ojp.usdoj.gov/bjs/cvict.pdf.

15. McGaa, *Mother Earth Spirituality*, 20.

16. Laura Mirsky, "Restorative Justice Practices of Native American, First Nation, and Other Indigenous People of North America: Part II," *Restorative Practices eForum* (May 26, 2004). Available at http://www.restorativepractices.org/library/natjust1.html Accessed January 15, 2006.

17. Howard Zehr, *The Little Book of Restorative Justice* (Intercourse, PA: Good Books, 2002), 50, 51.

18. Ronald Lessard, interview with the author, February 20, 2004.

19. Joseph Myers, The Criminal Justice Issues of Indian Country, *The Tribal Court Record*, (Spring/Summer 1996): 313.

20. Ada Pecos Melton, "Indigenous Justice Systems and Tribal Society," *Judicature* 79, no. 3 (November-December 1995): 126–133.

21. Ibid., 314–315.

22. Stewart Wakeling et al., *Policing on American Indian Reservations*, research report (Washington, D.C.: U.S. Department of Justice, National Institute of Justice, July 2001), NCJ 186185.

23. S. M. Manson et al., "Alcohol Abuse and Dependence Among American Indians," in *Alcoholism in America, Europe, and Asia*, ed. J. E. Helzer and G. J. Canino (New York: Oxford University Press, 1992), 113–130.

Chapter 3, Hinduism, pages 63-76

1. See Karen Pechilis, ed., *The Graceful Guru: Hindu Female Gurus in India and the United States*. (New York/Oxford: Oxford University Press, 2004).

Chapter 4, Buddhism, pages 79-95

1. Thanissaro Bhikkhu, written communication with the author, October 6, 2003.

2. Dharma 101," *Tricycle: The Buddhist Review*, http://www.tricycle.com. Retrieved August 25, 2003.

3. Rimpoche Nawang Gehlek, *Good Life, Good Death* (New York: Riverhead Books, 2001).

4. Karma Lekshe Tsomo, "Opportunity or Obstacle: Buddhist Views on Organ Donation," *Tricycle: The Buddhist Review*, 2, no. 4 (Spring 1993): 30–35, http://www.tricycle.com/issues/tricycle/2_4/feature/1601-1.html.

5. Acara Suvanno Mahathera, *How a Theravadan Buddhist Chinese Funeral May Be Conducted*, rev ed, (Penang, Malaysia: Sukhi Hotu, 1996).

6. R. Goss and D. Klass, "Tibetan Buddhism and the Resolution of Grief: The Bardo-Thodol for the Dying and the Grieving," *Death Studies*, 21 (1997): 377–395.

7. Gehlek, *Good Life, Good Death*, 69–70.

Chapter 5, Judaism, pages 97-112

1. Christopher Johnson and Marsha G. McGee, *How Different Religions View Death and Afterlife* (Philadelphia: The Charles Press, 1998), 145.

2. Neville Kirkwood, *A Hospital Handbook on Multiculturalism and Religion* (Harrisburg, PA: Morehouse Publishing, 1993), 49.

3. See national Jewish population survey based on 4.3 million Jewish households in Cathy L. Grossman, "Cultural Movement Kindles Interest of Secular Jews," *USA Today*, September 29, 2003, p. 8D.

Chapter 6, Christianity, pages 115-131

1. Adherents.com , *Top Twenty Religions in the United States,* 2001, http://www.urbandharma.org/udharma5/toprelig.html Available at http://www.gc.cuny.edu/studies/aris-index.htm

2. K. B. Bedell, ed., *Yearbook of American and Canadian Churches*: 1998 (Nashville: Abingdon Press, 1999).

3. Frank S. Mead, Samuel S Hill, and Craig D. Atwood, *Handbook of Denominations in the United States*, 12th Edition (Nashville, TN: Abingdon Press, 2005), 25.

4. E. W. Lidner, *Yearbook of American and Canadian Churches*: 1999 (Nashville, TN: Abingdon Press, 1999).

5. Mark Chaves, Mary Ellen Konieczny, Kraig Beyerlein, and Emily Barman, *The National Congregations Study*, page 26. Available at http://saint_denis.library.arizona.edu/natcong/jssrmeth.pdf , Accessed November 29, 2007.

6. Daniel J. Walkin, "Priests Campaign to Allow Clergy to Marry," New York Times News Service, May 1, 2004.

7. Center for Applied Research in the Apostolate, 2004. Available at http://www.cara.georgetown.edu Accessed on November 29, 2007.

8. James B. Smith, *A Spiritual Formation Workbook* (San Francisco: HarperSanFrancisco, 1993), 15–16.

9. Dennis T. Haynes, "Mormonism," in *Spirituality Within Religious Traditions in Social Work Practice*, ed. Mary Van Hook, Beryl Hugen, and Marian Aguilar (Pacific Grove, CA: Brooks/Cole, 2001), 251–272.

10. Ibid.

11. Francis X. Cleary, "Roman Catholicism" in *How Different Religions View Death and Afterlife*, ed. Christopher Jay Johnson and Marsha G. McGee, 2nd ed. (Philadelphia: The Charles Press, 1998), 193–204.

12. Richard M. Eyre, "The Church of Jesus Christ of Latter-day Saints," in *How Different Religions View Death and Afterlife*, 90–108.

Chapter 7, Islam, pages 133-158

1. Yvonne Y. Haddad, "Make room for the Muslims," in *Religious Diversity and American Religious History*, eds. W. H. Conser, Jr. and S. B Twiss (Athens, GA: University of Georgia Press, 1997), 218–261.

2. Jane I. Smith, *Islam in America* (New York: Columbia University Press, 2000).

INDEX

Order Form

Spiritually Sensitive Caregiving: A Multi-Faith Handbook can be ordered by check, money order, Visa, or Mastercard. Mail or fax this form, or call: **800-970-4220** to place your order. Outside the U.S. call: **828-675-5909.** You can also order on our secure website:

www.compassionbooks.com

1-9 copies: $12.95 each • 10-19 copies: $9.72 each (25% discount) 20 or more copies: $7.77 each (40% discount)

Shipping:

1 copy: $3.50 • 2 - 9 copies: add $.75 additional postage per copy. 10 copies or more, add 10% of total

Place my order for: _____ copies of *Spiritually Sensitive Caregiving:*

A Multi-Faith Handbook: $ _____

Tax: (NC only) 6.75% _____

Shipping: _____

Total: $ _____

Enclosed is my check or money order for: $ _____
Make checks payable to: **Compassion Books, Inc.**

Please charge my credit card (Visa or MC only)
Card # _____Exp. date _____
V#_____ (last 3 digits on back of card at end of signature strip)

Ship To: _____

Name: _____

Organization:_____

Address: _____

City/State/ Zip: _____

Phone/Fax: _____

Mail or Fax your order to: Compassion Books, Inc.
7036 State Hwy. 80 South, Burnsville, NC 28714

1-800-970-4220 / (828-675-5909) or Fax: 828-675-9687
email: bruce@compassionbooks.com • www.compassionbooks.com

For hundreds of carefully chosen resources to help with
grief and loss, comfort, hope, and healing
visit our website at
www.compassionbooks.com